"SERGEI WAS THE ONE WHO BROUGHT
LAUGHTER INTO OUR HOUSE. . . .

He brought the sun into my life. He taught me, who was always so serious, how to have fun. He took care of me without ever telling me that's what he was doing. Even now that he's gone, he's managed to look after me by leaving me Daria, who is so much a part of him.

"I want Sergei to know I will always take good care of her. She'll be the happiest girl ever. I'll make sure that she knows the kind of man her father was, the kind of heart he had. That's one of the reasons I'm writing this memoir now, before his lovely echo fades, as it inevitably will, with time. . . ."

—Ekaterina Gordeeva, My Sergei: A Love Story

THE CRITICS APPLAUD EKATERINA GORDEEVA AND *MY SERGEI* . . .

"Ekaterina Gordeeva writes of Olympic gold, love and sorrow . . . affecting, ingenuous."

—San Francisco Chronicle

"Of all the love stories written this century, few can rival the real-life tale of Russian pairs skaters Sergei Grinkov and Ekaterina Gordeeva. . . . Ekaterina Gordeeva has borne her sorrow with dignity, and through this volume, we now comprehend her loss."

—USA Today

more . . .

"Told with clarity and feeling. . . . Combines the dramatic reality of Gordeeva's life with an intriguing look inside the world of competition skating, and it's not surprising that the book has become a best-seller."
                                        —*Fresno Bee*

"Charming . . . The grace and beauty that Ekaterina Gordeeva displays on the ice comes through in her book. . . . Among the pleasures in this book are the multitude of photographs sprinkled throughout."
                        —*Mansfield News Journal* (OH)

"A beautiful and unique book . . . told with humor, civility, clarity and insight. . . . It has wit and many moving moments."   —*Ellenville Press* (NY)

"A beautiful love story and an inspiring testament to a person's ability to rebuild his or her life after tragedy."   —*Billboard*

"A LOVING TRIBUTE. . . . A vivid picture of their 'fairy tale' love story."
                        —*Milwaukee Journal Sentinel*

"EMOTIONAL AND HONEST, this book will grip the reader . . . tug at heartstrings."
                              —*Palm Beach Illustrated*

"Poignant, caring . . . Captivating."
                                    —*Library Journal*

My Sergei

A LOVE STORY

Ekaterina Gordeeva

WITH E. M. SWIFT

WARNER BOOKS

A Time Warner Company

WARNER BOOKS EDITION

Cover design by Diane Luger
Cover photos and title page photo by Heinz Kluetmeier
Cover photo colorization by Alexa Garbarino
Prologue photograph by Christopher Little

Warner Books, Inc.
1271 Avenue of the Americas
New York, NY 10020

Visit our Web site at
http://warnerbooks.com

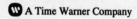 A Time Warner Company

Printed in the United States of America

Originally published in hardcover by Warner Books.
First Printed in Paperback: October, 1997

10 9 8 7 6 5 4 3 2 1

To Sergei

Я посвящаю эту книгу моему Сереже. Моему любимому, моему мужу, отцу моего ребенка, великому спортсмену и моему лучшему другу.

За свою короткую и богатую жизнь Сергей смог подарить многим людям прекрасные минуты. Он жил для земной любви и мог дарить ее людям, потому что это было естественное состояние его души.

Я благодарна Сереже за каждый прожитый рядом с ним день, за каждую его улыбку и доброе слово.

Сережа, я буду хранить нашу чудесную сказку, в которой мы жили, и расскажу ее нашей дочке !

—Ekaterina Gordeeva
1996

Я улыбаться перестала,
Морозный ветер губы студит,
Одной надеждой меньше стало,
Одною песней больше будет.
И эту песню я невольно
Отдам на смех и поруганье,
Затем что нестерпимо больно
Душе любовное молчанье.

—Anna Akhmatova
1915

Contents

Acknowledgments

For their sweet reasonableness during the brief but intense period when I was immersed in this book, I want to acknowledge the contribution of my family: Sally, Nate, and young Teddy.

And I would like to thank Katia, whose beauty comes from within, for her trust.

—E. M. Swift

My thanks and appreciation go to:

My parents; my sister, Maria; Sergei's sister, Natalia, for always loving and supporting me.

Ed Swift for his understanding and insight.

Jamie Raab for her energy.

Heinz Kluetmeier for his beautiful photos and generosity.

My dearest friend, Debbie Nast, who has been with me through difficult times and without whom my ideas will never come true.

Our coaches, Vladimir Zaharov, Stanislav Leonovich and Marina Zueva, without whom our successful skating life would not have happened.

All my friends for their love and support.

My little Daria who gives me strength and Sergei's Smile!

Special thanks to all photographers whose work is featured in this book.

—*Ekaterina Gordeeva*

Prologue

For me, a new life is coming, a different life from that which I knew. I felt it for the first time when I was back in Moscow, two weeks after my beloved Sergei's funeral. In my grief, I feared I had lost myself. To find myself again I did the only thing I could think of, the thing I knew best, the thing I'd been trained to do since I was four years old. I skated. I went onto the ice, which was always so dear to Sergei and me, and there, in the faces of young skaters training with their coaches, I recognized their bright dreams and hopes for the future. The new life is coming, I thought.

A little later, New Year's night, 1996, I was reminded of it again, this time in the sound of the laughter of my twenty-year-old sister, Maria, and that of her friends, and in my own laughter from being around them. How wonderful it felt to laugh, if only for a short time.

And always, especially, I feel stirrings of a new life whenever my daughter, Daria, is near. No matter how I am feeling, no matter where my mind is wandering in time, I have to smile back at her, because she is always smiling for me.

I have a picture of her father long before he became Sergei Mikhailovich Grinkov, two-time Olympic pairs skating champion. I seldom called him Sergei to his face. It was Serioque, which is softer, or Seriozha, softer yet, and more romantic, a name to be saved for special times. This picture was taken when Sergei was nine years old. He is skating on the ice where we trained as children. His face in the picture is Daria's face. She is four years old now, and has her father's shocking blue eyes, and the blonde hair he had as a child. She has Sergei's wide and ready smile, so beautiful to me. Sergei was the one who brought laughter into our house. He brought the sun into my life. He taught me, who was always so serious, how to have fun. He took care of me without ever telling me that's what he was doing. Even now that he's gone, he's managed to look after me by leaving me Daria, who is so much a part of him.

I want Sergei to know I will always take good care of her. She'll be the happiest girl ever. I'll make sure that she knows the kind of man her father was, the kind of heart he had. That's one of the reasons I'm writing this memoir now, before his lovely echo fades, as it inevitably will, with time.

Not long ago I heard someone ask a friend, If you had to live your life over again, what would you do differently? I've thought about this, and for me, I'd like to live my life over again backward. I'd like to live in a world where tomorrow would be yesterday, the day after tomorrow two days ago, and so on, because now I have little interest in the future. It's probably unhealthy for me to think this way, because of Daria, because I should be looking to the future for her. But it's true that any day I'm living now, I would exchange for any day in the past. I hope this will change with time. But I know that, for me, to find the kind of happiness I had with Sergei isn't possible. It's not unbelievably hard. It's impossible, like trying to find the comet that was in the night sky last spring, which passes Earth once in seventeen thousand years. No matter what lies ahead, the best years of my life will have been with my Seriozha, and those years are now laid to rest.

So I step into the future, as bravely as I'm able, with my heart longing for a time I'll never see again. With Sergei and me, everything was natural, almost inevitable. First we were skating partners. Then we were friends. Then we were close friends. Then we were lovers. Then husband and wife. Then parents. I lived in a world in which I always had my favorite thing to do, which was to skate. I had my favorite man around me all the time. I had my beautiful parents, Elena Levovna and Alexander Alexeyevich Gordeev, who wished for me only happiness. I never heard angry words from people, never experienced unkindness, because the one person I cared about loved me. I never looked closely at the world around me and examined it for flaws. I only paid attention to Sergei.

Then God took him away at the age of twenty-eight. Sergei died without warning of a heart attack on November 20, 1995, during a routine training session in Lake Placid. I lost my husband and best friend, the father of my daughter. I lost my favorite thing to do, because now I had no skating partner. The only thing God left me with was Daria. It was like He was sending me a message: Start your life over again, Ekaterina. Open your eyes to the world around you. Experience what it's like not to be so blessed. And this I now do. I am learning the disappointments of life.

Marina Zueva, who was Sergei's and my choreographer from the beginning, told me something after his death that I don't understand. Or maybe I understand it but cannot believe it. She told me she's not sorry for me.

Maybe she said this because I had such a beautiful life, and no one can expect such a beautiful life as I had with Sergei to last. Maybe because she's sure that I'll be okay. I don't know. I do know that I never thought that humans could handle so much. I never imagined people could be so strong, so resilient. Humans can handle any pain. Words, however, can cut the heart to the quick. Words can make the pain that never goes away. It's so true. And they can also make happiness that lasts forever.

I always felt Sergei was on a higher level than me, that he was stronger and smarter and more stable than me, and that he would always protect me. Now that he's gone, I feel vulnerable, unsafe in ways I never felt before. I'm scared to trust people. I'm afraid to say things, afraid that I may hurt people's feelings, or that people may say things that will hurt me. I never had any of these worries before. I find that I'm unsure of people's motives.

I never thought before I wasn't brave. I was always the first to jump from the heights into the water. Now it's like I'm out of my home for the first time in twenty-five years. It's like I was living in a fairy tale before, and now I've been abandoned in a wild forest.

That is what life was like with Sergei: a fairy tale. He was so honest and calm and solid. Sergei was a man first and then a skater. Not like me, who was a skater first, then a woman, then a mother. I wish I wasn't that way. I wish I'd saved more of my strength and power for Sergei and my daughter. I'm trying to learn to be more like Sergei, who was such a good father and gentle husband, strong and yet tender. I leave, and always did, too much of myself, too many of my feelings, on the ice.

I can't explain why, but I've started to make a list of things that Sergei wanted to do.

He wanted Daria to learn karate.

He wanted to skate in the Nagano Olympics in 1998. He had made one small mistake in Lillehammer, where we won our second gold medal. It was the only mistake that he ever made in a competition. The only one. He was so dependable, and he only missed this one time because he was worrying about me. So he wanted to compete again, to erase that single blemish from his thoughts. He kept this wish inside him for over a year before mentioning it to me. A third Olympic bid. I didn't think I could handle the pressure of another Olympics, but I couldn't say no, because I saw the hope in his eyes.

Sergei wanted to get a big globe of the world for our home. He loved to look at places we'd been, to study geography, and he wanted to be able to show these places to Daria.

He wanted his sister, Natalia, to visit us, and he wanted Natalia's daughter, Svetlana, to learn English. It was Sergei's great regret not to speak English, although he understood it very well. He was a perfectionist, and was too shy to speak until he could do it without any mistakes. Tutors in Moscow are expensive, about five hundred dollars a month, but Sergei said he'd pay for Svetlana's tutoring no matter the cost. She's thirteen, which he thought was a good age to learn.

He wanted to someday move to Idaho. To Sun Valley. We'd skated there a few times and both liked it very much. Sergei liked to ski. I loved the mountains. We loved the nature there, the forests, the beautiful night sky brilliant with stars. The wildlife and the great open spaces. This was a place for a family to dream.

He wanted to drive me through Europe. Or perhaps he would have taken me on the best train. He wanted to stop in all the cities, to visit the cathedrals and museums. He wanted to eat at the sidewalk cafes, to have wine with our lunches, and long naps in the afternoon when we were tired. He wanted to walk the boulevards while holding hands, to have no schedule to keep, or exhibitions to skate in, or competitions to train for, as we'd had for so much of our lives. No more rushing around without seeing. We talked of this trip many times.

I'm going to keep this list and add to it as I think of other things. Sergei wanted to do so much, so many different things besides skate.

Childhood

As I look back, I see that everything went too smoothly for me. I had no experience with the sadness of life. Even before I met Sergei, I was a happy child, innocent and naive, blessed with good health and much love.

My father, Alexander Alexeyevich Gordeev, was a dancer for the famous Moiseev Dance Company, a folk dancing troupe that performed throughout the world. He had strong legs and a long neck like a ballet dancer, and a stomach that was absolutely flat. Everything he did, he did fast, and he always moved quickly around the house. I can remember my father jumping over swords when he danced, bringing his legs up to his chin as the knifelike blades flashed beneath him, fourteen, fifteen, sixteen times in a row. Or he'd kneel down and kick, left and right, left and right, in the athletic manner of the folk dancers of Russia.

My father wanted me to be a ballet dancer. That was his big dream. He was disappointed that I became a skater. He had gray-blue eyes, the same color as mine, and a kind face. But he was also strict and serious, as if his kind face didn't quite match the words that came out of his mouth.

He met my mother, Elena Levovna, at a dance class when she was fourteen. They married when she was nineteen, and I was born when she was twenty. My mother was the sweet one, always perfect with children, the person I most admire on this earth. Selfless, generous, she was also quite beautiful as a young woman, five feet six inches tall, with a tiny waist and a very feminine figure. She walked like a ballerina, one foot just in front of the other. Her hair was brown, like mine, and wavy. Her fingernails were strong, and she polished them red and wore makeup every day. I used to watch in fascination as she applied it. She was always tender with my younger sister, Maria, and me, smiling much more often than my father.

She worked as a teletype operator for the Soviet news agency Tass. She was proud of her job, which paid her 250 roubles a month—more than my father made—and she liked to look nice when she went to work. She always wore high heels and beautiful clothes that my father had brought back from overseas, attire that set her apart from most Soviet women. She, too, traveled for her work. When I was eleven, my mother spent six months in Yugoslavia, and the next year she

My mother and me.

worked twelve months in Bonn, West Germany.
Even when she was based in Moscow, my mom
worked long and irregular hours, from eight in
the morning till eight in the evening one day;
then from eight in the evening till eight in the
morning the next.

So my maternal grandmother, Lydia Fedoseeva,
took care of me and my sister. We didn't have to
worry about day care or baby-sitters. We called
her Babushka, and she was an important person in
my life. She was short and a little heavy, but
walked very nimbly and was full of energy.

*With my father
in 1974.*

One time, when I was twelve, we were training at a place on the Black Sea, and one of the other skaters left my suitcase in the Moscow airport. The boys were in charge of the bags, the girls were in charge of the tennis racquets, and when I got off the plane, I had this boy's tennis racquet but he'd forgotten my bag. I could have killed him. So I called home to ask them to send my suitcase to me.

My grandmother went to the airport and picked up my bag, but she didn't trust putting it on an airplane by itself. So she took it on an overnight train to Krasnodar, five hundred miles, then took a bus to the resort where we trained. I got a call from the guard at the gate saying my bag had arrived. I went to pick it up, and there was my grandmother. I wanted to cry when I saw her. "Babushka, what are you doing here?" I asked.

She told me she had brought me my suitcase. She only stayed a few hours, then she walked to the bus and took the overnight train back home to Moscow.

Her hair was always short and neatly styled. When my grandmother was nineteen years old, her hair turned completely white, like paper, and ever since, she went regularly to the hairdresser. Her face was darling; her voice soft and soothing. I loved to listen to her read to my sister and me at night. My favorites were Grimm's fairy tales. Very, very scary. My grandmother did most of the cooking, and I liked to help her in the kitchen. She taught me how to knit and sew, and made my skat-

ing costumes for me until I was eleven. She taught
me how to suck the yolks out of eggs and decorate
the shells for Easter. That was one of my family's
favorite holidays. A few weeks before Easter
came, Babushka used to take a plate, fill it with
earth, then plant grass in the earth. She watered it
and tended it until the grass grew up. Then on
Easter morning we'd hide painted eggs in the
grass for my sister, Maria, to find.

My grandfather—my mother's father—also
lived with us. His name was Lev Faloseev, and I
called him Diaka, which is short for *diadushka:*
grandfather. He had been a colonel in a tank divi-
sion during World War II, a prestigious position
that enabled us to live in a lifestyle that was, while
not extravagant, quite comfortable by Soviet
Union standards. He taught about tank warfare at
the Red Army academy in Moscow. He always
wore a uniform to work, covered by a warm gray
coat in winter, and a big fur hat and strong leather
boots. His uniform always smelled very weird to
me, pungent and musty, so he took it off as soon as
he came home. Then he would have a nice long
dinner, followed by a glass or two of cognac.

He called me Katrine—nobody else called me
this—and he liked both me and my sister very
much. He was a calm man, a quiet man, who used
to let Maria and me play with his medals from the
war. We also liked to look at his books. I remember
thumbing through his history books and geography
books, which were very old and filled with maps of

famous battles, much more interesting than our fairy tales.

We lived in a five-room apartment on the eleventh floor of a twelve-story building on Kalinina Prospekt, near the Russian White House, where the parliament meets. It was a fantastic location, with a good view of the Moscow River. From the balcony we used to be able to watch the soldiers on parade march past our building on their way to Red Square. It was also a beautiful spot to watch holiday fireworks, which were aimed so they'd come down in the river. The Olympic torch in 1980 was also exchanged on our street. I remember watching the ceremony from our balcony when I was nine years old.

From what I could tell, I was the luckiest girl on earth, wanting for nothing. Like most children, I never thought much about the rest of the world. I never heard bad things about the United States, either on television or in school, was never frightened that someone would drop bombs on us, and never worried that the United States and the Soviet Union would go to war. It was more like: We're the happiest country; we're the greatest nation. I was fourteen before I began to learn anything about politics, and by then I understood, or started to, that when the government tells you something, it doesn't necessarily mean it's true.

❋   ❋   ❋

My parents used to vacation for a month every summer at the Black Sea. I hated to swim. I've always hated to swim, I don't know why. I'm not very good at it, and my mother tells me that the only time I ever got angry as a child was when I couldn't do something well. But in a roundabout way, a Black Sea vacation was how I got started skating.

On one trip my parents met a skater who trained at the Central Red Army Club. The club was known by its initials: CSKA, an acronym that we pronounced *cesska*. The army, like many trade unions in the former Soviet Union—automobile manufacturers, farm equipment makers, coal miners, steel workers—sponsored sports clubs throughout the country, and the biggest and most prestigious of these was CSKA. These sports clubs—and there were hundreds and hundreds of them nationwide—were quite professionally run, with the best coaches and facilities. They turned out the elite athletes that made the Soviet Union an international powerhouse in sports.

One key to the success of the clubs was identifying talented children at a young age and teaching them sound fundamentals so they could reach their full potential. Tryouts were held by age group, and they were open to anyone. Your parents didn't have to have any army affiliation to join CSKA. If your child was selected, the club was free of charge. It was affiliated with a sports

I started skating at age four.

school in Moscow that also provided the young athletes with an education. It was a great honor to be admitted to any sports club, but particularly CSKA, because sports was one of the few means by which a Soviet citizen could travel and see the world; and top athletes also got many privileges unavailable to the ordinary citizen, like hard-to-find Moscow apartments, cars, and relatively generous monthly stipends.

This skater knew of my father's dance company, and he suggested that my parents bring me to the rink at the army club in September to try out. I was only four years old, too young to start ballet and too young even to try out for skating. But this friend lied to CSKA officials and told them I was five, which was the age at which you were allowed to join. I was very tiny, which is an advantage for a girl in skating, and they took me right away.

It was impossible to find skates small enough to fit me in Moscow at that time, so I wore several pairs of socks beneath the smallest skates my mother could find. The first year I skated twice a week, a regimen that increased to four times a week when I was five. It was just an activity to me, something to give me exercise. I didn't have any goals in mind. If it hadn't been skating, it would have been gymnastics or dance. My mom never really believed I'd be anything special as a skater until Sergei and I won the Junior World Championships when I was thirteen. She just wanted me to be a normal kid and thought whatever I was doing was great. I never dreamed about Olympic medals or traveling the world like my parents. On the ice, I was not a good jumper. I just liked to skate.

But the Central Red Army Club had a long history of producing skating champions, and the coaches knew how to train a young child for future success. We did physical conditioning off the ice three times a week—abdominals, jumping, leg exercises—and ballet training three days a week, which I loved. We learned how to stand, how to hold our heads, how to hold our hands and arms. Everything. There was a mirror the entire length of the army club rink where we skated, so we could keep an eye on our posture. And I was always the smallest one, boy or girl.

My mother tells me that as a child I was obedient. I was not a troublemaker at all. And disciplined. In order to be at the rink by 7:00 A.M., which was when we had ice, I had to be up at 5:30 or 6:00 in the morning. Sometimes my parents wouldn't want to drive me to the early practice. I'd toddle in and wake them, insisting, "I can't miss it. It's my job."

This side of me came from my father. He was very hard on me, very demanding. He got mad at me if my hair wasn't braided, or if my shirt wasn't tucked in, or if my room wasn't neat; if my posture wasn't right, or if my face wasn't clean, or if my food wasn't eaten.

As a child I was always tense around my father. He expected me to be able to tell time when I was four years old. My mom always said, "It's all right, she'll learn it soon enough." She always had sympathy for me, probably because I was so tiny. But my father just kept on pushing me. I was scared of him. If he came to help me with my homework, my head didn't absorb anything because I was so afraid that I'd make a mistake. Always fast in mind and movement, he wanted the answers immediately. I got so stiff, so panicky, I couldn't do it. He expected the homework perfect, with no mistakes. If I didn't do it right, he made me repeat it again and again, until it was not just correct, but also neat. I used to make my sixes backward, and if I erased one of these mistakes, I had to do the whole homework sheet over again.

Looking back now, I can see that he was teaching me to strive for perfection. Sometimes I think he overdid it. But whenever I made a remark like "I want to finish first" or "I want to be the best," my father liked it.

Deep down, though, my father always had a kind heart. It's said that the eyes are a window to the soul, and I know it's true, because my father's eyes were kind. He sometimes came to my room before I went to bed and said, "Katia, I'm sorry I was so hard on you." He used to get angry with me if I got sick, saying it was my fault because I wasn't wearing warm enough clothes. I was even afraid to cough in front of him. But in the evening he'd come up to my room and give me my medicine, or would rub cream on my chest, and he'd apologize for getting mad.

He explained that he was the way he was because he'd always been hard on himself. He was already a dancer when he began serving two years in the army, and every night, after doing his army duties all day, he'd go to the ballet and work out so he wouldn't lose his conditioning. He told me, you always have to do extra. If your coach tells you to do five jumps, you must do eight. If everyone else does something once, you must do it twice.

Now I see my father with my daughter, Daria, and I can't believe he's the same man. He's so patient, and will take hours to explain something to her. If he asks her to clean up her toys, he will also help. I don't remember my father ever helping me clean up. When Daria was little, he would feed her the bottle and hold her as long as he could. He is completely different now that he's a grandfather. His body shape is different, too. Perhaps there's a connection.

School Years

I went to a sports school as a child. It wasn't just for CSKA athletes. There were also kids there from other sports clubs around Moscow. But everyone in the school trained in a sport in addition to taking regular classes. One of my classmates, in fact, was the hockey player Pavel Bure, who's now with the Vancouver Canucks.

Elementary schools in Russia have ten grades, and you start when you're seven and graduate at sixteen. We all wore uniforms. From grades one through eight, the girls' uniform was a brown dress with a black apron in the front. On holidays, the black apron was replaced by a white apron. At the top of the dress we wore a little white lace collar that was removable and could be washed separately, because the collar was always supposed to be clean. Then in grades nine and ten the uniform changed to a navy blue skirt and jacket, under which you could wear any color blouse. The boys, throughout, wore navy blue pants and jackets.

Then there were the pins. From grades one through three, we wore a pin on our shirts the shape of a red star that had a portrait of young Lenin on it. From grades four through eight, we wore a red scarf around our necks that signified we were members of the Pioneers, an organization something like the Boy Scouts. It taught us to respect older people, to be good citizens, to be patriots—that sort of thing.

In grades nine and ten, we wore a pin on our shirts in the shape of a red flag that had a portrait of old Lenin on it. That meant we were members of the Komosol, which is for strong young people who would help our country grow up. After that,

Sergei (in back) *in his school uniform.*

we graduated, and it was everyone's hope to some day be invited to become members of the Communists, which was a great honor. My parents were in this organization. To be a Communist, in Soviet society, was considered the highest level of good citizenship.

Classes went from September till May, and until I was ten years old, we had the summers off from skating. My favorite thing to do for vacation was to go to our *dacha*—a summer home an hour north of Moscow. We shared it with another family, and our part of the house had a living room, a small kitchen, and three bedrooms. It was in a village near the forest, and three miles from the dacha was a river where my father could swim. In most places this river was so shallow I could wade in it.

I loved being outside all day long. The train line between Moscow and Leningrad—now Saint Petersburg—was only a mile away, and five times a day the train roared through. We'd play on the tracks, or would sit on the nearby hillside and throw stones at the trains as they passed. The best game we played was War, where we built a camouflaged hut, and I played the nurse waiting for the soldiers to come back wounded. I'd bandage them up and send them back to the front. My father wanted me to spend this time stretching or running to improve my conditioning, but I just wanted to play. As I said, my father was a very serious man in those days.

I liked painting and coloring and crafts and playing with dolls. Very normal things. I used to chore-ograph shows for my sister at the dacha, creating lit-tle dramas to which we gave grand names like *The Last Concert* or *Borahtino,* the last of which is a Russ-ian fairy tale similar to Pinocchio. Then we'd invite the neighbors to come watch our production.

I'm afraid I was very tough on my sister when directing these shows, much as my father was tough on me. Maria was a cute and quiet girl who had very blonde hair as a child. She had round cheeks, pale skin, and wore her hair in bangs, so she looked a little bit like a boy. I would expect her to do certain ballet moves in the productions, even though she was four years younger than me and had never studied ballet. "So, you can't do this?" I would say haughtily, showing her a pirouette. I was domineering and very demanding.

But my favorite thing to do at the dacha was to pick wild mushrooms with my grandfather. He loved the forest, and had names for all the differ-ent places where we hunted for mushrooms. There was the Forest Across the River, or the Big Forest, or the Dog's Road. They all had different kinds of mushrooms that grew at different times of the year. One was a pine forest, where white mush-rooms grew. One was a birch forest, where orange mushrooms grew. September and October were good months for picking, but in June the biggest mushrooms came up, bigger than the biggest tomato.

Diaka would come in and wake me up at 6:00

A.M. My parents would still be asleep, because they came to the dacha for relaxation, and the last thing they wanted to do was get up early to pick mushrooms. Sometimes they slept till noon. My grandfather told me it was better to go early so the other mushroom pickers didn't get there before

*Me, my mother, and
my sister, Maria.*

you. It's a very popular activity in Russia. But if we were late some days, he told me not to worry; our mushrooms would hide from the other hunters until we came. And he was right, because we always found them.

Russian people have long looked at mushrooms as being mystical. There is a very old belief that says that once a mushroom comes under the gaze of a human eye, it ceases to grow. Diaka wouldn't let me carry a basket when we went hunting, because if the mushrooms saw you carrying a basket, they'd know what you intended and would hide in the grass and not show their faces until you had passed. And we never carried a knife. Imagine what you would look like to a mushroom, creeping through the forest with a basket and terrible knife. Very scary.

So Diaka would hide a plastic bag in the leg of my pants, and another in his pocket, and then the mushrooms would let us come near. We'd go far into the birch forest, and I'd try very hard to keep up with his long stride so the next time he would let me come, too.

When we had filled our bags and returned home, everyone would get excited, because Babushka would make nice dishes with our mushrooms. We cleaned them very carefully, washing them twice with a brush. Then my grandmother would begin to cook. In one dish, she would cut them up, blend them with onions, eggs, and spices, then make them into patties that she fried in butter. Or she would make a mushroom soup. Or she pickled them. I liked them pickled, and my grandmother would sometimes pickle a whole jar of only the smallest ones for me, because I, too, was the smallest. Unfortunately I hated mushroom soup. I preferred picking mushrooms with my grandfather to eating them.

Diaka would also take me fishing. He made a special pole for me, not too big, a very small one, and a bigger pole for him. Then we went to dirty places looking for worms. It's gross, of course, and maybe something I wouldn't do now, but when I was ten or eleven, I loved to put the worms on the hook. Red ones, ugly things, the bigger the better. We used them to catch carp. My father, too, sometimes went fishing for eels. He went at night to a place where he would shine a light into the water and then spear the eels as they swam toward it. Then he'd bring the eels home, and I'd help him smoke them in alder. Very, very delicious.

So, you see, it was a good childhood, filled with happy memories. I was skating singles then—the club did not put pairs together until the girls were at least eleven—and I was proud that my parents never came to my practices to watch. Many of the parents did that, and I always felt sorry for these skaters. You saw these kids later in their careers, and the first thing they did when they finished a program was look to their coach, then look up to their parents.

But my father always asked me about my practices. Every day. Which was why I always wanted to do well. I couldn't lie to him. If I did badly that day, I told him I did badly, and he would speak to me disapprovingly. That's why I used to hope that my Babushka would come to get me after practice, not my father. She knew I preferred it, and even though it meant she had to take two buses and the subway, she always tried to come get me. But often my father picked me up in the car, and if I told him it was just a normal day of practice, that was very bad. Definitely the wrong answer to give. If I said practice went okay, he'd say, "Explain to me how it was okay." He wanted to know every jump I tried and why I thought I missed it. Every night I had an exam.

If a young army club skater failed to show sufficient improvement during the year, he or she was not promoted to the next grade in the sports school. To give you some idea of how difficult it was, when I first started skating there were about forty kids in my class who skated at CSKA. By the time I graduated, just five boys and five girls remained.

The club always had a year-end competition that was like a final examination. My jumps were not strong, which is why I could never have successfully competed as a singles skater. The highest I ever finished in these competitions was third; the lowest was probably sixth. When I was nine, my father came to one of these competitions, which was held at seven in the morning. I was very nervous because my father was there, and when I was putting on my costume, I somehow zipped my hair in my dress. I started to skate, but I couldn't move my head. My ponytail was stuck in the zipper, lashing my head in place. Finally I stopped the program and went to the judge, and he let me unzip my hair and start over. Afterward my father had a very long face and big frown, and he didn't come to any of my competitions again until I was skating pairs.

My father's dream was still for me to become a ballet dancer, so when I was ten years old he asked me to try out at the central ballet school in Moscow. I did it only because he wanted me to. That's how obedient I was. However, I cannot truthfully say I tried my best. I went with a friend, Oksana Koval, who was also a skater and was a head taller than me. She passed, and I did not, because I was too short. Oksana is now a ballerina, but if she had not passed this test, it might have been she who skated with Sergei. Such is destiny.

My father was very disappointed in me when I failed the test, very upset, but my mother was a little relieved. She knew how hard it was to be a good ballerina, and how easy it would have been to fail after being selected. As for me, I wasn't at all concerned, because one of my skating coaches had told me, "Don't worry about this exam. You're going to be a great pairs skater." He had a talk with my father, too, and assured him that they would find a nice partner for me, and that I had a good future in skating. Still, my father wasn't happy. I was never quite good enough to please him. Maybe in the Olympic Games I was okay.

Sergei (right) was very tiny when he started to skate.

Sergei

The spring I turned eleven, my friend Oksana Koval and I were invited to skate on the large ice rink where the pairs and older boys practiced. Sergei was in this group. The coaches had told us to come and skate, it's no big deal, but my friend and I knew it was more than that and were proud that we were the only two selected. As we circled the ice, we gathered from the conversations of the other skaters that it was Sergei for whom they were seeking a partner.

That summer Oksana Koval joined the ballet school, and when I returned to the ice the next season, the pairs coach, Vladimir Zaharov, told me to come early to practice. He had chosen a partner for me. I was very excited because I knew it was going to be Sergei.

I had never spoken to him. I remembered seeing

him on the ice with the older boys, and also in school, and he was slender and narrow and handsome. But Sergei was so much older than me—four years, which at that age seems like a lifetime—that I'd never thought it possible that we'd someday be paired together. At school Sergei had caught my eye because he sometimes didn't wear the mandatory blue uniform like the other boys. He wasn't sloppy, though. He might wear a nice pair of slacks, a jacket, and maybe a skinny black leather tie that was in fashion then. He didn't carry a shoulder bag for his books like everyone else but preferred to carry a briefcase. It was very stylish and made him stand out from the rest.

He was a good singles skater—he'd been skating at the army club since he was five years old—but he wasn't a very strong jumper, which is why they asked him to try pairs. There was some question as to whether he had enough upper-body strength. Zaharov wasn't sure. Sergei's arms were tiny when we first started, so it helped that I was small. But once he began lifting weights, he quickly matured. I have some pictures of him in the place where we trained in the summer, called Isikool, and he was so beautiful. His upper body had already developed. But I was blind in those days and didn't notice. I only thought of him as a coworker.

He was always very quiet and shy, and didn't like to tell stories about himself. Last summer, a few months before he died, I said to him, "Seri-

oque? I must be getting older. You know how old
people are always thinking about their childhood?
I'm thinking more and more about my childhood."

He told me, "Don't worry, Katuuh. Me too. Let
me tell you a couple of stories about myself." Katuuh was the name he called me in casual conversation. Katia he only used when he was serious:
"Katia, we have to do the taxes today." And when
he wanted to call me his lovely, romantic wife,
then he called me Katoosha, very soft.

He had seldom talked about his childhood
before. Of course I knew that both his parents—
Anna Filipovna and Mikhail Kondrateyevich
Grinkov—worked as policemen in Moscow. It
may seem strange that the son of policemen with
no artistic background would become a figure
skater, but in the 1970s figure skating was very
popular in Moscow. It was a young and growing
sport, new to most people but shown so frequently on television that a lot of kids wanted to try.
And parents definitely encouraged their kids to
get involved in sports—any sports.

The Grinkovs were originally from the city of
Lipetsk, which is eight hours away by train. So
Sergei had no grandparents at home to take care of
him. Consequently his mother and father would
bring him to day care when he was a young boy—
six, seven, eight years old—to a place where the
children stayed all day and night. They'd drop him
off on Monday and pick him up after work on Friday. Sometimes his parents told him, "Don't worry,

Sergei, we'll be back to pick you up early, maybe on Wednesday or Thursday." He'd wait and wait, his little face peering out the window at the street, and when they didn't keep their word, he'd cry.

The other story he told me was that in the winter his parents sent him to some sort of camp where the children took their naps outdoors in hammocks—outdoors in winter. It must have been freezing. But the sun was so bright as it reflected off the snow that Sergei and the other children had to shut their eyes against it. Then they quickly fell asleep. If you slept well and didn't cry, afterward you'd get a piece of chocolate.

After he told me these two stories, he observed that he'd come out of it all right, so we needn't feel guilty about sending Daria to American day care, where we picked her up each day at noon.

Anna, Sergei's mother, has told me that she couldn't keep Sergei's clothes clean as a child. She'd change him for school, warn him not to get dirty, and the next thing she knew, Sergei would have fallen into a tub of water. I can't imagine that she took such a thing in stride. He never complained about his mother, but Anna is quite a serious woman, severe even, as one would expect of a Soviet policewoman. Nor was Sergei a model citizen at school. It wasn't that he was particularly naughty, or disrespectful, but Sergei hated conformity. And he despised hypocrisy even more. He didn't see why he should smile at someone he didn't like. He never understood why I tried to be nice to people, to everyone, even if they had done something to hurt me. We were very different in this way.

He lived on the very border of Moscow, in an apartment beside the Moscow River. It was the last street before it became another town, and you

Sergei on a camping trip as a young boy.

could actually swim in the river there. It was clean, and there was a little beach. Sergei liked the sea and swimming, which he always preferred to hiking. He liked to play all sports—tennis, soccer, hockey—and like most boys, he liked to play with toy soldiers. Anna told me he could sit in the bath for two hours with these soldiers.

I only met his father two times before his death in 1990, but Mikhail Kondrateyevich was very quiet, like Sergei, and also big and calm. It was from his father that Sergei got his character. Sergei's father was almost too huge to fit into his

Mikhail Kondrateyevich Grinkov,
Sergei's father.

car, and the first thing Sergei did when he had money was to buy his father a bigger automobile.

Their apartment had two bedrooms, a living room, and a small kitchen. Sergei's sister, Natalia, lived there as well. She was seven years older than Sergei and resembled him greatly—same eyes, same mouth, same shyness. He felt closer to Natalia than anyone else. With both parents working, Natalia was like a surrogate mother to

Sergei, and they looked to each other for company. Natalia could always handle pain, which, to Sergei, was the most important trait a person could have. To not show your pain. He was a stoic. He told me once that when he was five or six years old, he slammed Natalia's finger in the door by accident. They were playing some game, and she was chasing him. She grabbed her finger and ran into the bathroom to try to stop the bleeding, shutting the door behind her so Sergei wouldn't see the blood. She didn't want to scare him. It was quite a severe cut—she still has a nasty scar—but she never cried, and she never showed it to him until it had healed. He was still amazed at this years later, that she could be so strong. She's needed to be. Natalia's had a difficult life.

Like so many young Russians, she was married briefly and had a daughter, Svetlana, but the marriage ended in divorce. Divorce was very common in Russia in the 1980s, and one of the reasons for this was the lack of apartments. It wasn't possible to just buy an apartment. You had to go to the government officials, tell them you were married and living with your parents, that your husband was also living with his parents, and that you needed an apartment. Then you had to wait until the government gave you one. They put you on a list, but no one knew how long it would take. In the meantime, you had no privacy, you were living with either one set of parents or the other, and there was a lot of stress that usually led to divorce. That's what happened to Natalia.

❖   ❖   ❖

Zaharov was a great coach for beginning pairs skaters. He had been a pairs skater himself, from Sverdlovsk, which was the home of many very good pairs skaters. He knew the best way to do all the elements, the easiest way. We have a saying in Russia: It's stupid to reinvent the bicycle. I think that's one of the problems that pairs skaters have in the United States and Canada: they try to learn all the elements their own way, as if it's the first time it's ever been done.

Zaharov was basically a calm man, nice and quiet, who was patient when he explained things at first. Only later did he begin to lose his patience. He had olive-colored skin that became very tan in the summer, and also had blue, blue eyes. Zaharov was about forty years old, not very tall, but was strong and tough. I especially remember his powerful hands. He was so professional, and he could easily lift me off the ice to show Sergei the correct way to do the lifts. Sergei was just a teenager, and it wasn't at all easy for him. Zaharov used to make him practice all the lifts with a heavy chair made of iron, because a chair is quite awkward to hold, and so is a person.

As a pairs skater, you have to learn everything you learned as a singles skater over again. Even something so simple as a crossover is different, because now you are doing it with somebody else, and you have to align your body with theirs. We spent two hours a day on the ice for a week just learning crossovers. Poor Sergei, his legs were so much longer than mine that he was never able to take a full stride. His strokes were always shorter than was natural. We had to learn spins all over again, because now we had to do them in synchronization with all the angles of our bodies—our "lines"—aligned identically with each other. The death spiral was a very difficult element to learn. Both partners have to find the correct tension in their arms. One time I would lean back too far, the next time Sergei would lean back too far; and each time we'd collapse in a heap before the first rotation. My entire body was sore from learning the death spiral, which looks so effortless when it's properly done. But that's an illusion. The girl's abdominal muscles must be rigid the entire time.

We practiced the jumps endlessly. When you skate alone, you can jump whenever you're ready. But with a partner, you must do it together, right now, exactly, ready or not. The lifts, like every other move, are all technique, with each one requiring a different way of holding the hands. My hands used to get very sore, and to strengthen them I used to hold a bar with a weight attached to it by a rope, and wind this weight up and down. Sergei had to learn special steps so he wouldn't trip and fall when he carried me on these lifts. Zaharov taught us all these things.

I was never scared of the lifts, because I always felt very safe in Sergei's arms. His whole career, even when he was just learning, he fell on these lifts maybe three times. But the throws were terrifying to me. When doing a throw, the girl jumps at the same time as the boy throws her like a rag doll, gripping her by the arm and waist. Triple salchow throws, double axel throws—these were the elements Sergei and I performed. Propelled by the boy, the girl flies much higher than when she jumps alone. She travels farther in the air. We used to practice it on thick mats while off the ice, and when that was mastered, we'd move over to the rink. That was very, very scary. Zaharov would say something like, "Today we'll work on the spiral, some lifts, the spins, and then the throw." As soon as he said "the throw," I worried about it the entire session.

I fell repeatedly while trying to learn to land. I wasn't rotating far enough, or was opening my arms too late, or I didn't have my right leg bent and my left leg ready to reach out and point. It's difficult to know where the ice is when you're in the air after having been thrown. I kept falling and falling and falling. Sergei would say, "Don't you think you should go unlace your skates for a while?" That's what he used to do when he was tired: pretend there was something wrong with his boots. "Go sit a little bit," he would tell me. "I can't throw you anymore." I'd answer: "Why do I have to go sit? I'll just freeze and get more scared while

I'm waiting. I'd rather do it ten more times and get it over with."

So Sergei would throw me some more, and I'd keep crashing. He'd keep making the sad faces at me, hiding his eyes like he could no longer watch because it was too painful. But he never got mad at me. Some partners got angry and screamed when the girl didn't land the throws. Pairs skating can be very, very dangerous for girls. I've seen boys, exasperated to the point of cruelty, purposely throw their partners in a different direction than she expects, or throw her too high on purpose. This can be deadly. But Sergei was never like this.

I didn't cry. Maybe just a little, but I don't really remember. Stanislav Zhuk, who became our coach when we were a little bit older, used to tell Sergei, "You have to throw her as if she were a crystal vase." It may be true, but I wasn't very happy about this analogy. Why a vase? Why not a person? I'm not a vase. But maybe it helped Sergei throw me a little more gently. All I know for certain is that whenever Zaharov said we're going to practice the throw today, I got so nervous I wanted to be sick.

The other skaters in the club used to call me *BabaKatia*, which meant "little grandmother." I didn't particularly like this nickname, but they gave it to me because I liked to needlepoint. Also, probably, because I was very serious, very meticulous. Whenever we traveled anywhere, I always carried a bag with me that my grandmother had

packed that was full of everything a skater might
need if something went wrong with a costume:
safety pins, ribbons, rubber bands, scissors,
thread. Also little sweet cookies and candies and
snacks. My grandmother would tell me, "If you
don't want to eat it, Sergei will have it." She loved
Sergei, and used to make him pastries filled with
meat or cottage cheese, called *pirochkis*.

At the beginning of our second year together, in
September, Sergei missed a morning practice,
and Zaharov lost his patience. Naturally, I was
there. I never missed anything. If you told me to
go to the moon, I'd have gone there, too. But
Zaharov told me to go home and not come back
for the rest of the day. He said, "You don't have a
future with Sergei, and I'm not going to coach
him anymore. You, Katia, will keep skating as a
singles skater, and we'll look for another partner
for you."

I didn't think it was fair. I was proud to be skating with Sergei. He made me feel safe. He
seemed like an older brother to me, and I knew
he didn't miss any more practices than the other
boys. From what I remember, he didn't even miss
more than Zaharov. Sergei was just a normal
teenager who wasn't totally committed yet to
skating, wasn't sure if he was going to keep skating or not. But Zaharov pushed him hard, and
overreacted to Sergei's mistakes.

Zaharov called our parents and asked them to
come to a meeting at the club the next day. This, of

course, was unusual, so my parents decided to meet that afternoon with Sergei's parents to discuss the situation, before they saw Zaharov. It was the first time my parents went to Sergei's house. My father said that he thought Sergei was a good skater, that his body was nice, maybe not strong, but fine for only sixteen. But he thought he had to be more serious about training. They all wanted Sergei to realize he had done something wrong by missing too many practices. So my parents waited at his house, and when Sergei got home, he was shocked to see them sitting there. The first words out of his mouth were "Where's Katia?" because I'd stayed home from the evening training session. He still didn't realize how upset Zaharov was at him.

My parents told Sergei to call me at home. He phoned, and he and I decided to meet the next day at the subway before practice and talk things out. That was the first time we'd ever met off the ice together, and I was very upset, crying, because I knew how angry Zaharov was. I knew that Zaharov wouldn't coach Sergei any longer, and the idea of changing partners scared me. I'm not sure why, but I always believed Sergei was the only one who could skate with me. It had nothing to do with having romantic feelings toward him. I thought that he was a very attractive man, of course, but since I was so little, and he was so much older, I never thought he'd have special feelings for me. But I'd always imagined it would be fun to be around him.

Our first program choreographed by
Marina Zueva, 1982.

Not that anyone asked my opinion. It's only in America that they worry about how the skaters are feeling. For us, it was always, "Go ahead and skate. It's too bad for you if you don't like it."

When he met with our parents later that morning, Zaharov spoke very bluntly. He said I could not skate with Sergei, because Sergei wasn't very good as a partner. Sergei's mother said, "Fine, we'll leave CSKA and go to another sports club, and Sergei will become an ice dancer." She always thought pairs skating was the hardest discipline because of all the lifting the man had to do. Also, in ice dancing there was no jumping. But my parents, who knew my feelings, told her I was not going to skate with anyone else. They thought the decision of whether we stayed together or not should be mine and Sergei's to make. Not Zaharov's. It was then that Sergei and I made the commitment to skate together, to become a team.

So Zaharov left us after coaching us one year. Our new coach became Nadezheda Shevalovskaya, a woman who also worked at CSKA. She had an old friend, a former ice dancer, who was studying to get a degree in choreography from the National Theater Institute in Moscow, and Shevalovskaya asked this friend to create a couple of programs for Sergei and me. In this way, the incomparable Marina Zueva came into our lives.

We were young, she was young, and Sergei and I became Marina's project. In order to graduate she had to present a finished program to a panel of her teachers, and we skated this program for her. It was done to music sung by a boy's choir, very romantic and light, with no throws to worry about. Still, I was nervous the day her professors came to the rink to judge Marina's choreography. But Marina told us then, and repeated it to us often over the years, "Don't worry about the judges. They're just people who want to enjoy your program. They're happy they're not going to the office, so try to help them enjoy it."

When Marina first started working with us, she was skinny, with long black hair that hung straight down. Her fingernails were red, which I liked, and her fingers were long and slender. She touched you softly, and it felt good when she tried to help you fix some little movement. After she was with us a couple of years, she started to pay attention to fashion, and I was always amazed how she could change her look completely overnight to stay in style. She made many of her clothes herself, and they were always tasteful. She wore leggings and long sweaters in the mid-eighties, when they were the style elsewhere. But in Russia it was very radical for a woman not to wear a skirt. She cut her hair and dyed it red. She was a pioneer who wasn't afraid of what people would say. In those years, if you stood out, people would talk about you. That's all changed now, of course. Now the people in Russia can't spend their money fast enough to keep up with the fashions. It's crazy. But everything was different then.

As she created a program, she'd describe every movement for us. She'd tell us why we were holding our hands a certain way. Why she wanted it soft. Why it should be strong. She'd bring a picture of something onto the ice and would say, Do this pose for me. Copy this picture. Or she would say, How would you act out spring? Do flowers, birds, love, sun. Now show me winter. Or, Make this shape for me on the ice. Sergei would laugh sometimes at these exercises, because Marina always used unusual words. She might say, Go run across the ice like a little animal. And she worked with us a lot on our expressions. We would stand in front of the mirror and make faces at ourselves for hours after practice, sometimes from 7:30 to 9:30 in the evening. Marina would ask, How would you be funny? How would you be sad? And we would show her.

The programs tended to be very difficult when she first made them, and then she'd have to take things out to make them skateable. For instance, she might ask us to clap twice during a crossover, turn our heads, then do a difficult jump. Impossible. Sergei would say to her, Marina, will you show us? Can you do this first, Marina? Or, Marina, it's not possible to close your eyes before you jump.

We finished sixth in our first Junior World Championships, which were held in Sapporo, Japan, in December of 1983, three months after we had started skating with Shevalovskaya. The next year, when the Junior World Championships were held at the Broadmoor in Colorado Springs, we won them. Sergei was seventeen years old and I was thirteen.

It was our first visit to the United States, and to us it was like a little fairy tale. It was Christmas and there was a lot of snow, and Christmas trees decorated with beautiful ornaments. I took two of these ornaments home for souvenirs, a gold one and a navy blue one; I stole them right off the tree. There were candles all around, and Santa Clauses. And when the snow stopped falling, it was suddenly sunny, just as in a dream, all the snowflakes sparkling like crystal. The Broadmoor had a little pond with ducks in it, and Sergei and I would walk out and feed the ducks. I couldn't believe how beautiful it all was. Then the weather got warm, and I was amazed that in winter you could walk outside without your jacket.

Everyone had warned us that the skating would be difficult because of the altitude, and one of the skaters before us came off the ice coughing blood. But it didn't turn out to be a problem for us, and we skated clean, which our coaches had told us was the most important thing. Don't try too hard, they warned. We weren't expected to win, and after we did I remember going to a toy store to celebrate. There was a little monkey on sale for six dollars that I loved, and since, for me, it was a lot of money, I made a trade with the shopkeeper for a *matroishka* I had brought with me, one of those stacking wooden dolls that are made in Russia.

Another early program choreographed by Marina.

Then I asked Sergei to trade another matroishka for a turtleneck sweater. It was very difficult at that time to buy children's clothes in Moscow, so I was always careful to bring home the same number of gifts for my sister that I bought for myself. I bought us both a pair of pants and a shirt, plus warm boots for Maria and a long blue winter coat for me. The coat cost sixty dollars, which was a fortune. But it was something I could never have found at home. For my friends I always brought back souvenir soaps, shampoos, and lotions from the hotel to give out as little gifts.

After the competition there was a banquet, and what I remember best was Sergei staying around the girl ice dancers, all of whom wore beautiful dresses. He didn't pay much attention to me off the ice. We were not very close friends yet and I was very young, both in years and in experience. For example, on the plane ride home, I sat with Vladimir Petrenko, who was Viktor's younger brother and my age exactly. We ate ice cream, and this was unbelievable to us, beyond the realm of possibility, how they could keep ice cream frozen for so many hours on the plane.

Sergei turned eighteen on February 4, and, for the first time, I gave him a gift. It was a key chain that my father had brought back from Spain. It had a little gun on it that could shoot caps, and although this was a small gift, I was so shy that I worried about it endlessly. But Sergei liked it and kept it with him, which made me happy.

That spring we competed in a Friendship Cup at a beautiful mountain resort in Bulgaria. After the competition our team went outside together, and we were playing in the snow, having fun, throwing snowballs. Sergei loved that kind of horseplay. It was then that, for the first time, I remember becoming aware that I found him attractive, and that it was nice to be with him.

I never told anyone these feelings. To my great regret, I never had any close girlfriends to confide in. Maybe if I had been spending more time at home, I'd have talked about my feelings with my mom. But we were so often at training camps or competitions that I spent more time with Sergei than I did with my family. Among the other skaters in our club, Anna Kondrashova was the girl I spent the most time with, but she was seven years older than me. To Anna, I was a child. Most of my life was like this. I was seldom around kids my own age.

I had to try to figure out all these mysterious feelings on my own, which I was not equipped to do. I knew that I felt sad sometimes, but I always thought I was sad because I was homesick. Not because I was lonely. I was so disciplined about training when I was thirteen, fourteen, fifteen, sixteen that I never went to a friend's house just to talk and gossip and do stupid teenage things. That's the age that girls discuss boyfriends and crushes and feelings. It's a void in my life I'll never be able to fill.

And that's one of the reasons I was so attracted to Sergei. He always had friends around him. He could go wherever he wanted and do whatever he wanted to do. His life seemed very different from mine.

The Miserable, Pitiless Zhuk

*I*n May 1985 I turned fourteen. Sergei was too shy to come to my birthday party, but he called me on the phone to ask if we could meet. We settled on a spot near the subway, a short distance from my house. I was obviously excited. As I mentioned, Sergei seldom spent time with me off the ice. When he arrived at the meeting place, he had with him a huge toy dog, white and light brown in color. It was quite expensive. Looking back now, remembering how seldom Sergei ever surprised me with gifts, I'm amazed he had the courage to buy me this wonderful present. Afterward, this dog was always in my bed.

Marina Zueva had created a difficult short program for us for the 1985–86 season, which was done to music by Scott Joplin and involved lots of footwork and pantomime with our faces. Sergei had a nice, understated way of acting, using very natural expressions that never distracted from our skating. Marina used to have me watch Sergei and try to do what he did. They thought alike. She was closer to Sergei than to me, because he was older, and also because he shared her interest in reading. In her eyes, I was always the little girl, too small for some of their philosophical conversations.

Marina also made a difficult long program for us to a medley of music by Duke Ellington and Louis Armstrong. The music was much more sophisticated than what other pairs were skating to, and we liked it very much. But the choreography was hard. In an early competition that year, Skate Canada, I fell as we did our side-by-side triple salchow, a challenging jump that Shevalovskaya had added to our elements.

The head coach of the army club at that time was Stanislav Alexeyvich Zhuk, who by any definition was a miserable, pitiless man. After my mistake, Zhuk told Marina that I had fallen down because it was a bad program. He would create a new program for us, one that was plain and simple and showcased only elements, not choreography. He also said that he was coaching us from now on, not Nadezheda Shevalovskaya. Thus began the longest year of skating that Sergei and I ever endured.

Zhuk, too, had been a pairs skater, finishing

second three times in the European Championships from 1958 to 1960. He was in his mid-fifties,
short, with a big stomach and a round face. His
most arresting feature was his eyes, which were
small and dark and looked very deep into you.
They were very scary, peering at you from
beneath his hairy eyebrows. All of Zhuk's movements were fast. He also had very strong but not
very nice hands. I didn't like it when he showed
us movements with his hands. And on the ice,
when he demonstrated something to us with his
feet, he couldn't straighten his leg. It looked
ridiculous.

Sergei used to laugh at Zhuk, but not to his
face. We used to imitate the way he walked fast,
taking very small steps. Sergei didn't like him as a

Sergei and me with Alexeyvich Zhuk, 1985.

person. Zhuk drank every night, and he used to speak harshly, even filthily, to the boys. He liked to order them around as if they were soldiers, because they skated for the army club. "Shut up," he would say, "I'm higher than you in rank." Zhuk liked these army rules.

We used to skate in the morning from 9:00 to 10:45, then afterward we'd spend forty more minutes practicing lifts. Then I went to school, did my homework, and came back for the evening practice from 6:30 to 9:30.

Sergei had finished high school, and during the day he liked to take a nap. But Zhuk believed you should not sleep for more than forty-five minutes in the afternoon, or you would be too relaxed to train well that night. Our good friend Alexander Fadeev, the singles skater who also trained with Zhuk, used to sleep for three hours in the afternoon. So did Sergei. As a result Zhuk started telling people that Sergei was lazy and undisciplined. That he didn't listen to the coach. That he missed practices. He told me that I should change partners because of Sergei's habits.

I hated him when he said that. I always believed Sergei was the only one who could skate with me. I never, ever thought I'd change my partner. But Zhuk kept telling me bad things, and he had an expression he liked to use, accusing Sergei of "infringing on the regimen."

It made Zhuk furious that Sergei didn't take him seriously, that he just ignored him off the ice.

Sergei used to say to Zhuk, "After practice, what I do is none of your business. If I want a beer, I'll have one. If it's Saturday and we don't skate, I won't get up at 7:00 A.M."

Zhuk could have told me anything, and I would have done it. I was, if nothing else, obedient. So I worried that Sergei wasn't doing what he needed to be doing to become a champion. This was stupid of me, because in fact Sergei was lifting weights to make himself stronger and was skating beautifully. No matter what he did—tennis, soccer, running— Sergei was always very competitive with the other boys. He had his own code for living. Even though he never told anybody this code, he always lived by it. Sergei knew what was right and what wasn't. I knew only what I was told.

Zhuk's goal seemed to be to keep us as busy as possible, and to keep us around him as much as possible. Maybe because he was very lonely. Maybe because it was the only way he could keep himself from drinking. Zhuk wanted to control our lives. He used to tell us, "If I don't coach you, you'll never be on the World or Olympic team." He tried to make us completely dependent on him, to make us think he was the only one who could look after our health and teach us how to eat and sleep.

He had us keep journals: how many jumps we attempted, how many we landed, how many throws, how many spins; how we felt before practice, how we felt afterward. Every night we were supposed to update these things. Sergei wouldn't do it. He'd take my journal and copy it. But of course I kept mine scrupulously. I was so good about it. We had to bring our journals to practice every day so Zhuk could see that we were doing them properly. And every month we'd have to add everything up—how many hours altogether on the ice, how many jumps, how many landings, how many misses. Very, very scary.

In the summers Zhuk had two places he liked to take us for off-ice conditioning. One was to a resort on the Black Sea, with a very mild climate, sort of like South Carolina or Virginia. We'd go there in mid-May and early June. We'd meet at 7:00 A.M. every morning, and Zhuk would tell us what lay ahead for the day. Then we'd run from 7:15 till 8:45, always on a normal road, never a special track, and never a special distance. Zhuk would just say run over there and run back. Do it twice, or whatever. Sometimes we'd run along the beach, on the rocks and shells and sand, which was uncomfortable but probably good for strengthening our ankles.

At 9:00 A.M. we'd have breakfast, then we'd do exercises that were good for the arms. We'd go to a special place near the sea that had big, round rocks, and we'd take these rocks and throw them forward, backward, and to the side. It was supposed to make our jumps better. The rocks weighed about five pounds, and we'd throw them back and forth fifty, sixty, seventy times. Zhuk was always very specific about how many repetitions. And of course I always did them exactly as he ordered. Then maybe we did some pushups and situps.

The worst was running the stairs. Zhuk always took us to places that had stairs. The longest was 225 steps; another had 175 steps. Sometimes he made us not run, but jump up the stairs, first with one leg and then with the other. Always with a stopwatch, and always we'd have to record what we'd done in the journals. Then at night, at our evening meeting, he could say "Today you were better" or "Today you were worse; we'll have to do something with you."

Zhuk also thought that undersea diving was important for skaters. Snorkeling. He said it helped you control your breathing. You learned to take a deep breath and to hold it. But in skating, you don't have to control your breathing. Only Zhuk, this madman, thought you did. I remember once in the middle of May he told everyone we were going spearfishing with him. It was his favorite hobby. Naturally I was the only skater to show up, and I was so angry at the others for not telling me they weren't going to come. Just me and Zhuk. It wasn't summer yet, and the sea was cold as ice. I was freezing. He told me to put some clothes on over my swimsuit, so I would be warmer. So I did. The flippers were too big because they didn't have a small enough size for my feet, so I added a couple of pairs of socks. I put on a sweater, warm pants, and even a warm hat. I hate the sea anyway, and since I don't swim well, it was so scary. Then Zhuk went into the water with his speargun and made me follow behind him.

In July, when the weather got hot and humid, Zhuk used to take us to Isikool, a health resort in the mountains. I preferred this place to the Black Sea, even though the altitude made the training on the stairs very difficult and painful. There was a beautiful, deep lake at Isikool about which there were lots of legends, and in the afternoons we used to go on long hikes through the woods. We played soccer and tennis, and sometimes Sergei and I would play mixed doubles together. Although he was always very competitive when he played with other boys, he was never competitive with me. I, however, used to get upset when I made a mistake, and Sergei would laugh and shake his head and ask me what I was getting upset about. We were supposed to be playing to have fun.

The best time for Zhuk was when we were training on the ice at Navagorsk, a center for elite athletes that was thirty minutes from Moscow. Navagorsk was in the country, surrounded by forests. It had more than one hotel, each with its own cafeteria, plus soccer fields, a movie theater, a swimming pool, a gym, a physical therapy center, and of course an ice rink. It wasn't just used by skaters. Athletes in soccer, volleyball, and basketball also trained there. We used to go to Navagorsk fifteen days before every important competition: Nationals, Europeans, and Worlds.

For Zhuk it was ideal, because every night, instead of going home to our parents, we were in the hotel, and he could call a meeting. He always found some business to do: either listening to music or going over the journals or talking about what we were going to do the next day.

I was homesick all the time. I often cried myself to sleep at night. I shared a room with Anna Kondrashova, and Zhuk would tease us about eating dinner at the cafeteria. Anna always had a problem keeping her weight down, so we stopped going to dinner because afterward Zhuk would tell such stories about how much we ate and how much we'd weigh if we kept eating dinners like that. Just the girls he'd tease. So instead we'd skip dinner and would walk fifteen minutes to town to buy fruits, vegetables, and candy. Lots of candy. As I'm writing this, I can hardly believe what I'm saying. What were we thinking? How did we listen to him?

One time I saw Zhuk hit Anna. I was in the bathroom, and Zhuk came and started talking loudly to her. I decided I'd better stay where I was, but then they started fighting, and when I came out, he was hitting her on the back. I ran out to get Sergei, but by the time we came back Zhuk was gone. Anna was crying. That was nothing new. She cried almost every day.

Zhuk used to come to her and say, "I saw you

last night go into Fadeev's room. What were you doing in there?" Even if she had done this, it was none of his business, of course. But he would torment her with his spying, and I was so young that Anna never confided in me what was behind it. I understand now that he was trying to get Anna to sleep with him. He had done this with many girls over the years. Not me, fortunately, because I was so young. He had enough power that if a girl refused him, he could arrange it so she couldn't skate anymore. This was a man without a heart.

Maybe being around this man is what made me, not a strong person, in the way my mother is strong—but a tough person. Tough enough to handle anything. Tough, not in a good way, but in a way that allows you to handle the bad things that life throws at you. Tough but hard. Too hard sometimes.

The 1986 Nationals were held in Leningrad, and it was the first time Sergei and I had competed at the senior level. We skated well, but to be honest I didn't even worry about missing an element, because we were so perfectly trained. In my opinion we were overtrained, with nothing else in our heads. We did side-by-side double axels, triple salchow throw, double axel throw, triple twist. We finished second to the defending world champions, Elena Valova and Oleg Vassiliev. But Zhuk told us we had skated better than them. "That's okay," he said. "You'll be first at the Europeans."

The Europeans were held in Copenhagen that year. Before we went, Zhuk made me go see an acupuncturist, who puts needles in special places to make your pain go away. I don't know where he found her, but her real magic was discovering the weakest point in your body. She called it a hole. She found such a hole in me, right beneath my left shoulder blade. I had not known this place was a problem until this woman told me it was, and pushed into this place until it hurt. She claimed she could see through my whole body through this weak point. It was my most vulnerable spot. The funny thing was, it wasn't like I had a problem this lady was fixing. What kind of a problem do you have when you're fourteen years old? The only problem I had was I didn't have enough time to play with my dolls. That was the problem. But this lady could see a weak spot on my back, and she could touch it, and sure enough, because I had trained so much, it was a little bit painful. This was a very bad hole. She gave me a special metallic disc to put over the hole, which she said would protect me. She attached it with a piece of tape. Now I was prepared for the competition.

Then guess what? I lost it when I took a shower. And I thought, Oh no. That's bad. I'll fall down. I'll miss all my elements because of the exposed weak hole beneath my left shoulder blade. We were already in Copenhagen for the European Championships, and I was distraught. Then right before the competition I found the metallic disc on the hotel room floor. So I put it back on, and all was saved.

Zhuk told Sergei and Fadeev to come to see this lady, too, but they just laughed at him. He couldn't force them. Sergei never took any of it seriously. He was only serious with Zhuk during practice. And of course he was right. It wasn't that he ever caused a problem for Zhuk, or raised his voice, or told him off. He just knew that off the ice, his private life was his own. He would do everything Zhuk said on the ice, but that was it. He was not obedient like me, who would do everything anyone said.

Zhuk did, however, help me with my confidence. No one had expected us to be at the European Championships in 1986. They didn't even have our names listed in the program, which Zhuk took pains to point out to us. He told me, "You will skate clean." But I already knew that. And I was absolutely certain about Sergei. I never, ever worried about him. Even in practice I couldn't miss anything, because whenever we missed something during our practices, Zhuk made us do it over again. It was like my father with the homework. Only instead of doing it once, we'd have to do it three times. I learned the double axel this way. Zhuk would tell me to do five double axels in a row. And if I did four in a row and missed the fifth, I had to start over. Always Zhuk had us practice a specific number of jumps.

We didn't feel any pressure at the European

Championships in Copenhagen, where we again finished second to Valova and Vassiliev. But we skated our programs without a mistake. After the free program Elena Valova was crying so hard, because she knew we skated better than she and Vassiliev, even though they won. She was having a lot of problems with her leg and wasn't healthy enough to skate her best.

The trip to Copenhagen seemed more like a holiday to me than a competition. The queen of Denmark came to the Sunday exhibition and gave us huge boxes of Danish chocolate. We went shopping, and I remember buying some red boots that I later wore to the World Championships in Geneva. Every day we got twenty dollars in living money, and I used it to buy jeans that actually fit me, which were impossible to find in Moscow.

I could see clearly that life was nicer in every way in the West than it was at home. The streets were cleaner, the food was better, the service was quicker and more friendly. It was totally different from what we were used to—it was a nicer life but a more expensive life. I always brought gum and nice fruits home with me. During the winter it was impossible to get oranges and apples in Moscow. I also bought souvenir T-shirts for Maria and pins for my grandfather.

As soon as we returned home, we had to start preparing for the Worlds. There was no chance to recharge. You're so weak after a competition from the travel and the emotional letdown that your body is susceptible to illness, and I came down with the flu. Then Sergei and I had to keep doing our programs in practice, the same ones we'd skated so well at the Nationals and the Europeans. Again and again and again, always under Zhuk's critical eye.

So when we arrived in Geneva for the 1986 World Championships—our first—it wasn't with the carefree spirit we'd had before the Europeans. It was like going to work. I was more tired and nervous than I'd ever been before, and the whole competition I could think of only one thing: I wanted to go home and be with my mom. I missed her so much.

Before the free program Zhuk told Sergei to take me for a walk, and we went to Lake Geneva to feed the swans. Sergei asked me if I was nervous. I said I was. And he said, "Yeah, me too." But he didn't look nervous. He always looked so calm, and to see him always made me feel calm, too. We didn't talk much, and we didn't touch each other. We still had an age barrier between us.

We skated cleanly again, and when Valova and Vassiliev made some mistakes, for the first time all year we beat them. In our first try, we had won the World Championships. I couldn't believe it. I didn't even like the program that Zhuk had created for us. There was no theme, no choreography. The movements didn't mean anything to me. The music was not classical, not jazzy—it was almost like restaurant music, except there were funny, childish noises near the end of it, almost like a passing train. What Zhuk had us doing with our hands had nothing to do with what we were doing with the rest of our bodies. We just proceeded from element to element without feeling, intent only on not making mistakes.

I was, strange as it sounds, disappointed. It was our first trip to the World Championships, and we won. As we stood on the winner's stand, I remember thinking, Why are they giving me this medal? These are the World Championships, the ones you only watch on TV. I never dreamed of being an Olympic or World Champion. And suddenly I was one, but somehow it didn't feel right.

I went back to the hotel, sat down on my bed, and cried. It was too easy. It gave me no satisfaction. I cried and cried. Anna Kondrashova looked at me and said, "What are you, crazy? You were great." But I wasn't happy about it.

Sergei went to the fountain in Lake Geneva the next day and wrote his name on it. He only told me about it years later, saying in his teasing way, "Oh, you didn't go with me? Too bad."

That spring we performed with the other medalists on a twenty-city tour sponsored by the International Skating Union (ISU), through Switzerland, France, and Germany. We traveled by bus, and despite the fact that it was our first such tour, looking out the window was the only fun thing about it, thanks to Zhuk. I passed the time doing needlepoint. It was very boring, and the skating was difficult. Zhuk made us do either our short or long program every night, because we had no exhibition numbers—the fun, often frivolous programs that skaters prepare in case they're asked to perform in a show. They're never as difficult as competition programs. But Zhuk made us do all our throws and jumps. The buildings where we skated, in places like Davos, were cold, and we never had a chance to properly warm up.

Zhuk roomed with Sergei, and he would follow Sergei around, spying on him, never letting him go anywhere by himself. Zhuk gave trouble to all the Soviet skaters, refusing to let us go to the discos with the others. He told us that if we did, we'd never be Olympic champions. The worst thing was, I was so disciplined that even if someone had asked me to come along, I wouldn't have gone.

Brian Boitano, who was also on this tour, later told me that he and Alexander Fadeev, whom everyone called Sasha, went for a walk one day, and Sergei came along. Brian asked Sasha, who spoke English, to ask Sergei what he loved about skating. Sergei said that he didn't love skating. He skated because he had to.

That feeling in him eventually changed. But at the time I suppose it was true. It was so depressing to have to listen to Zhuk every day. He put pressure on us the whole season: from Nationals to Europeans to Worlds to the tour. It's why I don't like the memory of our first World Championships.

Strolling in a Moscow park in fall 1986, shortly after
our first World Championships.

Little Attentions

$\int$ ometime during the summer of 1986, Sergei, Alexander Fadeev, Anna Kondrashova, and Marina Zueva prepared a letter to send to Central Red Army Club officials asking that Zhuk be removed as head coach. He had become intolerable, drinking for days on end, missing practices, and becoming increasingly abusive to the boys. He wasn't fit to be coaching anyone, old or young. They asked me to sign it too, which I did.

My father was angry. He said to me, "This wasn't your idea. Why can't you think for yourself? Make up your own mind rather than allow yourself to be influenced by the others." He was right about one thing. I am a Gemini. I tend to look at something one way one day, then the opposite way the next. I am too influenced by the opinions of others. But not in the matter of Zhuk. I despised this man every day. My father, however, thought that Zhuk was a great coach, figure skating's equivalent to the legendary father of Russian hockey, Anatoly Tarasov. If he had a problem with drinking, he believed it could be solved.

Sergei, however, had made his decision. He talked to my father several times that summer, just a few words, but he told him he had to change coaches. Under no conditions was he going to train with Zhuk anymore. I remember overhearing them on the street one day, talking very seriously, and Sergei telling my father, "She's going to skate with me, and I'm going to decide what coach we'll have." Sergei never told me, "Don't worry, I'll take care of you," but I always felt it was so.

My father's attitude started to change after we finished second in the Skate Canada competition because we weren't well prepared. Also, Zhuk had driven me to tears in August when I wanted to go to our dacha one weekend to pick mushrooms with my grandfather. We had no training time scheduled. Zhuk said, "Fine, Katia, but first come over and we'll listen to some music for a new program. It will only take a couple of hours and then you can go." So I went, and it took all day, and we didn't have time to go to the dacha. He upset me so much, and when I saw my father I couldn't hold in my tears. Which was when my father finally said, That's enough.

It was an awkward situation for the entire Central Red Army Club, since Zhuk carried the rank of a colonel. Armies the world over like to protect their own. The generals who oversaw CSKA finally decided that Zhuk could keep his title as head coach, but that Stanislav Viktorovich Leonovich would coach us, and travel with us, and otherwise be completely in charge.

Leonovich had won a silver medal in pairs at the 1982 Europeans with his partner, Marina Pestova. For one year we had trained on the same ice together at CSKA, and I had always called him Stas. Now that he was our coach, I began calling him by his first two names—Stanislav Viktorovich—which is more formal and respectful. He was a nice man, a kind man, with an interesting face. He had a cute nose, almost like a duck's nose, and it made me want to smile just to look at him. Although Sergei and I were so happy to be rid of Zhuk, my father worried that Leonovich wasn't tough enough to be our coach. He didn't think he had enough experience.

But under Leonovich, everything changed, and skating became enjoyable again. The first thing he did was to bring back Marina as our choreographer, and she resurrected the Duke Ellington number that she'd made for us in 1985, the one that Zhuk had not let us skate because it was too difficult. It became our free program that year.

This number had more dancing, more footwork, more choreography, and more fun than anything we'd skated to before. Marina, Leonovich, Sergei, and I used to be the envy of all the other skaters because we had such a good rapport on the ice, always laughing and enjoying ourselves. When Sergei missed a practice, as he still sometimes did, Leonovich never raised his voice. Instead of get-

With our new coach, Stanislav Viktorovich Leonovich.

ting angry, he would say, "Do you understand that because of your absence, Marina, Katerina, and I weren't able to work yesterday?" Leonovich always called me Katerina—he was the only one to do so—because he thought it would make me feel older. He'd say, "There is more than just you, Sergei, who's involved." And Sergei understood this reasoning, and he stopped missing the practices. Rather, he stopped missing them alone, because as we grew older, he sometimes taught me to skip a practice with him so we might go fishing or waterskiing together on the Volga River. He never forgot there was more to life than the ice.

We won the Nationals for the first time that season, then went to the 1987 European Championships in Sarajevo. That summer we had learned a very difficult move called the quadruple split twist, in which Sergei threw me in the air, I did a split, then closed my legs and made four turns before he caught me. We were the only pair to do this quadruple element, and it was very exhausting—more exhausting than difficult, really. Soviet doctors had measured my pulse rate as exceeding two hundred beats per minute when I did it. I had to spin so fast that one time my elbow caught Sergei in the eyebrow, and within a few seconds his eye had swelled closed, and the next day it was a grisly black and blue.

Sergei turned twenty on the day we skated the long program at the Europeans, which we would long remember because of an unfortunate occurrence. In the first minute we had successfully done the quadruple split twist, which even Scott Hamilton, who was doing television commentary, incorrectly identified as a triple. So did most of the judges, which is one of the reasons we dropped this element from our program before the Calgary Olympics: it expended so much energy but didn't appreciably improve our marks. Then somehow the elastic strap at the bottom of Sergei's pants broke.

This strap was flapping around Sergei's ankle. It wasn't a danger, because it had snapped back up and was not dragging on the ice. But the referee, Ben Wright, an American, started blowing his whistle because he was worried that Sergei would trip.

We heard the whistle, but we didn't know that it meant for us to stop. And with the triple salchow throw coming up, I was much more concerned about that. When I landed it perfectly, all the most difficult elements were behind us, and we naturally wanted to continue. Zhuk had always said to keep skating no matter what is happening around you, and only listen to your coach.

Then Ben Wright had the technicians turn off our music. It was eerie, to be skating in a full arena to complete silence. We looked over to Leonovich, but he made no sign for us to stop. "Skating?" I asked Sergei. "Yes, we're skating," he said quickly. So without our music playing, we continued our program, which was very tiring because of the concentration required. We had never, ever practiced our program this way. But we were skating well, no mistakes, and the audience began clapping for us long before we had finished. Afterward we were exhausted and very confused.

The judges were instructed not to write down our marks. The Russian judge told Leonovich that we could skate the program over again after two more pairs had skated, giving us a short time to rest. But neither Sergei nor I wanted to do this. We didn't think we could skate any better than we just had, and we didn't understand that if we didn't skate again, we'd be disqualified. So when, after two more pairs, Leonovich asked if we were ready, we told him no. We were all done. He should have pushed us more, but Leonovich was never pushy. Sergei just didn't want to skate it again, and neither did I. We were disqualified from the Europeans.

This was a sign of Leonovich's inexperience. First, he should have told us to stop skating when the whistle blew. Then, he should have insisted that we try again, no matter how tired we were, knowing that the judges would surely mark the defending World Champions leniently after such an unfortunate incident. But it was a mistake the three of us shared responsibility for, and it made us angry as we prepared for the 1987 World Championships in Cincinnati.

Ben Wright was at the Worlds, too, and he apologized to us for what had happened. We said that we, too, were sorry and did not hold him to blame. In Cincinnati we skated our free program, this time to music, as well as we were able. In fact, of all our competitions, the 1987 Worlds may have been the time when we skated our best. We successfully defended our title, and this time, when it was over, I had no impulse to cry.

Afterward we went on our first American tour with promoter Tom Collins, a nice man who puts on a show every year that features exhibitions by the World and Olympic champions. He has an exclusive arrangement with the ISU, and the skaters—who in those years were all amateurs—love to be invited on his tour, which plays to packed arenas throughout North America. According to ISU rules, we were only allowed, I think, eight hundred Swiss francs a year in cash payments, but Tom always gave us extra money, maybe fifty to a hundred dollars a week. We weren't supposed to talk about it. But it was enough for me to be able to buy a four-hundred-dollar TV for my parents before I went home. Sergei helped me pick it out at a store in New York that was owned by a Russian sailor. He also helped me choose a suitcase in which I could carry all the clothes that I bought for my sister and me, and all the gifts for my parents and grandparents. Russian skaters always had huge luggage problems on the flight home.

My English at the time was almost nonexistent. I had taken English in school but had missed many classes because of skating, and I didn't even remember the alphabet. Sergei and I would go into a restaurant, open a menu, and have no idea what anything was. It made me self-conscious all the time.

My roommate on that tour was Tracy Wilson, the Canadian ice dancer, whose partner was Rob McCall. She was older than me, and I think Tom Collins wanted her to watch out for me. She ordered room service every morning and always asked if I wanted something too. If I said yes, she never let me pay for it, no matter how hard I tried.

During this tour, I always sat with Sergei on the bus. He read quite a lot, while I looked out the window or did needlepoint. It was new for me to spend time with him off the ice. He would sometimes come to my room and ask me to go for a walk, or to go with him for dinner. We didn't have much money, so it was just to McDonald's or maybe a pizza place. Sasha Fadeev was also on this tour, but Sergei still went with me.

Maybe he was just taking care of me. I didn't know. He always helped me with my luggage and offered me a hand when I was stepping off the bus. But this was just the way he was. He also offered his hand to the next lady stepping off the bus. He was a gentleman, and I think maybe he learned this from watching Leonovich, who was the same way. Leonovich had always treated his partner, Marina Pestova, with respect. He believed that how partners got along with each other was as important as how they looked in practice. If everything was all right off the ice, everything would be all right on the ice, too. Leonovich, I think, was too kind to be a coach.

When we were in Los Angeles, Sergei and I went to Disneyland with Sergei Ponomarenko and Marina Klimova, who were married. It was just the four of us, and Sergei was very happy that day, in such a good mood, always laughing and being funny. He bought me some ice cream. A couple of times he hugged me after a ride, or put his arm around me when we were standing in line. He had never done this before, and it made me excited. This was a wonderful day for me.

The tour went to twenty-five cities and lasted a month. So many new experiences. In New York Tom Collins got us tickets for *Phantom of the Opera*, and beforehand we ate dinner at Sardi's, which had all the pictures of celebrities on the wall. Another time Sergei and I danced together at a place with a jukebox, but not just the two of us. There were four or five of us dancing in a group. Sometimes, after we had skated and were waiting to go out for the finale, Sergei would hug me in the hallway, but never if someone was watching.

I didn't think much about these little attentions. At least I don't remember reading too much into them. A couple of times Sergei and I went to the movies, and we held hands during the show. I don't know why that was such a big deal, since we held hands all the time on the ice. But this was different. This was nice. I remember how hard my heart was beating when he reached over and took my hand. Afterward I didn't say anything. I just smiled at him. I never asked why he was holding my hand. All I knew was that it felt great.

I figured it was only because he was excited to be on this tour and was feeling so good that he did it. I didn't think it had anything to do with me. I assumed when we returned to Moscow, he'd go back to being the same way he'd been before.

Yet things changed after that tour. My mother, who adored Sergei, began to invite him to the house all the time. She loved how he played with our Great Dane, Veld. It was now easier for me to give him things, and even flirt with him a little bit if he was in the mood for it. It wasn't like I was planning anything or had any great designs to capture his affections. Sergei and I never planned anything, ever, more than two days ahead of time. Especially about our relationship.

American women, I think, plan much more than Russian women. At least the Russian women who grew up in the seventies and eighties, before the breakup of the Soviet Union. American women have much more to plan for. Not only must they try to find a life partner who's a doctor or lawyer or businessman, but he must be good looking, too.

In Russia, everyone was more or less on the same level. There was very little difference between being rich and poor. So if you found someone you liked, or loved, the next question was only when the marriage would be. Not whether he could make a good life for you or was a suitable match for you.

There was no need for elaborate planning. Today, of course, it is different, and Russian women know how to look for a good businessman with money to marry the same as Americans do. But I never had such notions in my head.

A Holiday Wish

For training purposes, it was now an Olympic year. I was sixteen, Sergei was twenty; and everything became focused on that single goal.

Our preparations began in June 1987, when we went to Sukhumi in Soviet Georgia for twenty days, which is where Marina started to create two new Olympic programs for us. Our support staff was larger than it had ever been. We had a special conditioning coach to oversee our running and lifting. We had a team of doctors who checked our weight every day and tested our blood several times a week by pricking our fingers. Heaven knows what they were looking for. We ate better food. The figure skating federation gave us caviar every day, which was high in protein and low in fat.

We'd begin each day with a morning workout

before breakfast. We ran and lifted before lunch. In the afternoon we worked with Marina. Then we had another workout at 5:00 P.M., before dinner.

After a week at home, in July we went to a place

Pre-Olympic training, summer 1987.

higher in the mountains, Sachkadzor, in Armenia, so we could train at altitude. I always liked these training camps, even though we worked hard. It was pretty in the mountains, and on our days off we had a chance to go hiking or take picnics. We were there with a lot of different athletes—boxers

At training camp, getting in shape for Calgary.

and gymnasts and handball players—and in the hallway of the dormitory there was a big calendar that listed how many days were left before the Olympics, summer and winter.

It was a much more intense atmosphere than usual. All the skaters were there, not just those from the army club, and the coaches were always timing our runs. I was never any good at these races. My times were abysmal. Zhuk was there, too, but fortunately not as our coach. He still sometimes worked with us in an overseeing capacity, though, and one day I twisted my ankle badly when he had us practicing the quadruple split twist off the ice after I was already tired.

I told Sergei that anytime he wanted tea or coffee after dinner to come to my room, because I had an electric kettle. Or if he wanted to eat something sweet. He didn't come often, but a few times he did, more to drink tea or eat a sweet than to see me. But it was a good feeling to be able to share these moments with him.

If I went to the market to get fruits, I was always sure to get something for him, too. Sergei was too lazy to go to the market, but sometimes he bought me ice cream in the afternoon, which was wonderful for me. We never went alone, however. Sergei always had older friends around him, like Sasha Fadeev. But it made me happy to be included.

Sasha was short, very muscular, with strong legs and a strong upper body. His eyes were tiny; his lips were tiny; his hands were tiny. Everything about him was tiny. But he was very quick when he skated, and he used to jump like a rubber ball. He was very, very talented, but in my opinion he never fully realized his talent.

Off the ice, however, everything about Sasha was unbelievably slow and relaxed. If you asked him the time, you had to ask him three times.

"Sasha, do you have the time?"

"Huh?"

"Do you know what time it is?"

"Hmm?"

"What time is it?"

Then he would tell you. When you talked to him, he would be thinking about the last subject when you had moved onto the next one. He was also stubborn and independent. If everyone went into a restaurant and ordered one type of pizza,

Sasha Fadeev

Sasha would be sure to order another type. He was proud to be different.

Yet he was always very, very kind. Sasha used to catch me furrowing my brow when I was listening to him or Sergei. I was so little that I looked up to everyone, and as I did this my brow became furrowed. He'd use his fingers to smooth the wrinkles from my forehead. Everyone did this to me. It got to be quite embarrassing.

The next training camp we went to was in Dnepropetrovsk, in the Ukraine, where we trained on the rink where Oksana Baiul learned to skate. That's where, for the first time, we skated our Olympic programs. Because it was an Olympic year, the entire federation watched us to give their approval. I liked the free program Marina had made for us immediately, which was to a medley of music by Chopin and Mendelssohn. Marina told us we were supposed to be fresh and springlike, to skate as if we were looking at the blue sky from beneath apple blossoms. That's why our costumes were sky blue, with sprigs of white flowers sewn over the shoulders.

The short program was from the opera *Carmen:* "The March of the Toreadors." Many of the members of the federation thought it was too serious for us, that the music should be more romantic. Marina, ever the iconoclast, told us not to worry, it would be fine. Still, I couldn't help but listen to the comments, and, like a good Gemini, I worried about this program one day and was confident about it the next. We changed the beginning many times before the Olympics, but kept the music. The program required us to act the part of toreadors marching before a bullfight, displaying all the beauty, grace, and pageantry of that passionate event.

We bypassed the early competitions held in North America—Skate America and Skate Canada—so the team doctors could monitor our health as closely as possible. The Soviet Union's sports machine left very little to chance. That was okay. The goal, we knew, was the Olympics; and as the Games approached, everything became a little more stressful, a little more intense.

In mid-November we won an event called the Moscow News. Afterward there was an exhibition, and while practicing for this exhibition, Sergei caught his blade in a soft rut in the ice. While holding me aloft in a star lift, with my hands and legs fully extended outward, Sergei dropped me. The first part of my body to hit the ice was my forehead.

I didn't feel any pain at first, then my entire head felt like it was splitting apart. Someone picked me up, I think it was Leonovich, and then I blacked out. I came to in the first-aid room, and I was driven to the hospital.

I ended up staying for six days. I'd suffered quite a serious concussion. I lay there worrying about missing practice and the Olympics, and I was mad at Sergei because I thought this fall was his mistake. Then there was a knock on the door, and it was Sergei.

He was carrying a dozen roses, and he was very, very upset. It was the first time he'd given me flowers. I was surprised, even happy to see how distressed he was. Many boys—and I'd trained on the ice with a few—would have been happy to drop their partners on their head. Spending so much time together training can lead to intense personality conflicts, and successful pairs are not necessarily friendly. But Sergei was so sad that I began to feel sorry for him. He stayed in the hall after giving me the roses, and it scared him when they wheeled me out of the room in my bed so I could go have some tests. That night he had to return to the Moscow News exhibition to pick up our trophies, and the pictures in the newspapers the next day showed him looking quite sad. His obvious distress had a buoyant effect on my spirits. Sergei visited me three more times before I got out.

I had another visitor, too, who brought me flowers. He was a friend from school, Valery Kharlamov, the nephew of the famous ice hockey player of the same name. I only mention this because he was the only other person in my life who could have passed for a boyfriend, although that was because he wanted to be my boyfriend, not because I wanted it. I never had very fond feelings for him, although I did go with him to a movie once. Sergei only saw us together one time, and it was interesting, because he got very upset. Valery and I were sitting together on a bus on the way to my practice, and Sergei also got on this bus. I was embarrassed when he saw us. And afterward, Sergei didn't want to practice. He began teasing me, saying, "Maybe you have to go already because someone is waiting for you." He was definitely jealous. It was a bad day for both of us.

After getting out of the hospital, it was another week before I was allowed on the ice, and Sergei continued to visit me at home every day. When, at last, I could skate again, I immediately noticed a change in the way he was holding me. He was holding me tighter, as if he didn't want to give me a chance to touch the ice. It was like he grew up during this period when we didn't skate. I felt more secure. Something had happened in those two weeks, and even I—so focused on skating, so serious about training and life—realized that his thoughts for me had changed. Before we had been like two skaters. After that, we were a pair.

Because of the training time I had missed, the figure skating federation told us we didn't have to compete at the Nationals, which were held over Christmas, in order to represent the Soviet Union at the Olympics. And that year, for the first time, my family invited Sergei to celebrate New Year's Eve with us.

In our family we never used to celebrate Christmas on the twenty-fifth. The thirty-first of December was the big holiday celebration. On the twenty-eighth or twenty-ninth my father would get up very early in the morning so he could buy the best Christmas tree, because they brought them from the forest to Moscow during the night. He'd bring it home, and when my sister and I were very small, my father and mother would wait until we were asleep to set up the tree. Then they would decorate it during the night. When we awoke the first thing we saw was this magnificent Christmas tree standing in our apartment, beautifully dressed in ornaments as if by magic.

Once Maria and I were older, though, we also helped in this wonderful project, and on the thirtieth the family decorated both the tree and the apartment. On the thirty-first my mother and grandmother would start to cook the Christmas meal, maybe fish, maybe duck. It was something different every year. I liked to help them cook. We'd make cold cuts and salads and cut up exotic fruits that had been saved especially for Christmas.

We always had a special bag under the tree, which we called the Santa Claus bag. My grandmother sewed this bag, which was red and white with a big white ribbon on top. It was beautiful. For a couple of days before New Year's we'd slip presents into the bag until it was huge. No one was supposed to see you putting the gifts in, so it would look like the bag was growing, growing, growing. Then at midnight, after drinking champagne and wishing each other happy Christmas, happy New Year, we'd open the presents.

It was actually my parents' idea to invite Sergei. I told them no, he wouldn't come; he had his own friends. But I asked him anyway. He said he'd try to come, but it was still a surprise for me when he showed up. I thought maybe he'd sit with us for a while and then leave, but he ended up spending the whole night with us.

He was a little shy at first, because it was his first time with our family like this. It was just Sergei, me, my father, mother, sister, and grandparents. We had a lot of candles around, and everything was beautiful, because Christmas is the most beautiful holiday all over the world. For a gift I gave Sergei a needlepoint picture I'd done of a clown with a wide smile painted on, and little tears coming down his face, sitting on a bench feeding the birds. He was very happy and surprised. This needlepoint is still hanging in his mother's apartment. But he protested at first, saying, "No, I don't need a gift." Probably because he didn't have anything for me.

I don't know where my mother got this idea, but she told us that at twelve o'clock exactly she was going to take an old plate and drop it on the floor, so it would break into little pieces. Then, before the twelfth toll of the clock, everyone had to grab a piece and dash off to hide it somewhere in the apartment and make a wish. If someone were to find this broken piece during the year, they weren't supposed to touch it, or the wish wouldn't come true. Even if one of us was cleaning the apartment, we had to leave the piece alone. So we had to hide them very well.

It was the first time my family did this. My mother dropped the plate at the first stroke of midnight, and we all scrambled to grab a piece and ran away. I don't remember where I hid my piece, but I do remember what I wished. I wished I would skate well in the Olympics. And I guess it came true.

That year the European Championships were held in Prague. I still wasn't in very good condition. Since my fall, I'd lost some weight and strength, and I was still having headaches. I wasn't eating well, for whatever reason, and was nervous about everything. Sergei and I didn't skate our best, but we won anyway. I missed something—a jump or a throw, I don't remember—and I was so upset, as if I'd done something terrible. Sergei said, "Don't worry about it. It's not the Olympic Games yet. We'll be ready in time."

But at that championship it became clearer than ever to me that Sergei felt more responsible for me on the ice. I liked it very much. I'd always been a little nervous about whether he'd pay enough attention to training, but now that I wasn't as strong as I should have been, Sergei had become stronger, more secure, more serious. I felt that despite my weakness, Sergei would take care of me. During the Europeans we ate breakfast, lunch, and dinner together. Then, after we had won, we danced together at the banquet. It was a fast dance, but it was the first time I remember just the two of us dancing. Sergei never really liked to dance.

Then we went to Navagorsk for the final preparations before Calgary. The whole Winter Olympic team was there, and the doctors checked our blood pressure and weight every day. I was down to eighty-four pounds, having started the season weighing ninety. I felt okay, but I was very stressed out and tired. I couldn't relax or eat properly. I think because all season everyone was so serious about the Olympics, because we kept being tested by the doctors, because the coaches kept telling us we had to be in the best shape of our life, I just assumed I should lose weight. The Olympics, I believe, are a year-long celebration of the nerves, and I was too young to understand what it was doing to my body.

I remember having lots of meetings at Navagorsk where team officials went through the schedule with us many times, and talked about the spirit of the Olympic Games. They told us about Canada, how we had to be a team, to help each other, be more friendly with each other, take care of our health—all this stuff. I don't think anyone was listening. I didn't like it, because they were taking up time when we could have been resting.

Then we were given our Olympic uniforms. I got boots for the opening ceremonies, but they weren't my size, so I saved them for my mom. This happened to me all the time. The skirt and jacket they gave me to wear were huge, so huge that not even my grandmother could tailor them to fit me. I looked terrible in them. I was always so jealous of the Canadian and American teams, because they always had sizes that fit even the tiny girls. Meanwhile I was wearing these big ugly things that made me look like a bag lady.

As the day of departure neared, everyone began giving me advice. They were all so worried about me because I was so young and tiny. It was driving me crazy. "Did you ever read this book?" someone I barely knew would ask. "Maybe you should read this book." It got so crazy that after all the waiting, all the hard work and training, when the day finally came to leave for the Olympic Games I didn't want to go. I missed my mother so much. We'd been training in one facility after another, and going from one competition to the next, and I felt almost like I'd been taken from my family against my will. It really surprised me, but all I wanted was to stay home with my mom.

Calgary

*O*n January 27, 1988, we flew to Montreal, spent the night, then took a morning flight to Calgary. Sergei held my hand the entire plane ride. It's strange, but it didn't mean anything to me. It was just nice, and I was a little proud to have his hand on mine. But I was so focused on myself, so consumed with the thought of the Olympics, that it didn't say anything to me about his feelings. I should have been in heaven, but I was quiet and withdrawn, thinking only of our training. Maybe that's why everyone was so worried about me and always giving me advice.

After picking up our credentials, we drove to the nearby town of Okotoks. It was more than two weeks before the opening ceremonies, but our coaches wanted us there early to get accustomed to the time change. It was a quiet town, and we stayed at the Okotoks Inn, a cute, small hotel. It was very cold, but there wasn't a lot of snow.

Townspeople came to our practices every day, which presented some problems. It's tough to have people clapping when you're trying to work on an element. Practice isn't supposed to be a performance. You're concentrating, then another skater makes a jump and suddenly there's a burst of applause. I found it very distracting. But the people were certainly nice, and the first day one of the spectators gave me a doll.

Sergei's twenty-first birthday was on February 4, and they presented him with an ice-cream cake after the morning practice. Elena Valova gave him a card that showed a stork bringing something in a blanket, and when you opened the card you saw it was a bottle of liquor. He could now legally drink. For luck, Sergei wore a gold chain around his neck with a horseshoe charm, and I gave him a pendant with the Calgary Olympic symbol on it to wear on this chain. I was nervous about giving it to him, and afterward everyone teased him: Whooo, Katia gave something to Sergei. But it made me happy when he wore it.

The ice dancers arrived in Okotoks a week after we had, and Tatiana Tarasova, who coached the team of Natalia Bestemianova and Andrei Bukin and would one day coach Sergei and me, brought me some gifts from my parents: chocolates, a letter, and a picture of them with my sister, Maria. And caviar. When athletes from the Soviet Union

A difficult element from our short program.

traveled, we always carried extra caviar, and it was invaluable when bartering for Levi's, music tapes, or cash. But in Calgary we didn't have any caviar to trade, because when the team officials gave it to us, they opened it. They wanted us to eat it for the protein.

We moved into the Olympic Village on February 8, which was beautiful and very well laid out. Each time we went in we had to go through security, and they checked our bags carefully, which took a long time. It took forever if we were on a bus. Also, all the women athletes had to go through sex control, to make sure we were really women. They took a little scraping from the inside of your cheek, examined it in a lab, then gave you a card that said you had passed.

Sergei got a bad stomach flu and a fever the day we moved into the Village, and he became so ill that he couldn't skate for two days. The speed skating doctor put him in his own room to tend to him. It was scary for me. This doctor, whose name was Viktor Anikanov, wouldn't let Sergei eat anything for two days. Sergei was so pale that I was worried he wouldn't be able to compete. But by the third day he'd recovered and was fine.

About the only thing I was eating was cheesecake. The cheesecake they served in the athletes' cafeteria was the best I'd ever tasted, and every day that was my meal. I ate salad, too, and maybe yoghurts and fruit. But no meat. Nobody told me not to eat meat, but I'd decided on my own that I was not going to eat it. In fact, everyone was telling me to eat this and this and that too, worried that I was too thin, and it was driving me crazy.

Because the boys were living on a different floor from the girl skaters, I didn't see Sergei as much as usual. I was rooming with Anna Kondrashova. Once in a while I'd bump into Sergei around the Village, and he'd be with Sasha, who was his roommate, or with some other friend. But I didn't feel comfortable just coming up to their room and talking to them, or sitting with them if they were already eating. Elena Valova and Oleg Vassiliev were nice to me, but because I was so small they would tease me with remarks like "What are you eating?" or "Why don't you eat anything?" I didn't feel like listening to it. So I'd go to meals by myself and eat whatever I wanted. I wrote in my journal that I missed home very much. There I was, about to compete in the Olympics, and all I wanted was to go home. Can you imagine?

The ice rinks in Calgary presented some problems. The Saddledome, where the competition was going to be held, was huge and comfortable and had a regulation Olympic-size surface. But it was seldom available to us for practice, since so many hockey games were being played there. So we practiced every day in a Canadian-size arena, which was shorter and narrower than we were used to at home. Sergei and I had to be careful not to hit the boards all the time, and it was unsettling to go back and forth between these different-size ice surfaces.

We had decided not to march in the opening ceremonies, since the short program was the following day, and we had a practice that afternoon.

Mike Powell/Allsport

After skating our free program.

Instead, we watched them on television. The next morning the head coach of CSKA, Viktor Ryshkin, visited to wish us luck. We felt close to him, and it was great for my morale to see him. He also brought me hugs and kisses from my parents, plus candies and still more caviar and another letter from my mom. Reading it brought me lots of energy. I now remembered who I had to skate for: my parents, who had given me so much. I also wrote in my journal that today was my first Valentine's Day, which in North America, I'd been told, was when lovers exchanged gifts. But it wasn't a holiday for Russians, so Sergei and I didn't exchange anything.

I was confident. I can't explain why. All the waiting was finally over, and I think the anticipation had been what was making me crazy. The short program, the toreador march, went almost perfectly, and we were scored first. The only problem, a small one, was when we finished we had our backs to the judges. We looked up and—oops—no judges. We'd lost our bearings during our final spin. But we just laughed a little bit and turned around to make our first bow, and no one knew about this mistake except us.

I'd already decided how I was going to celebrate when it was over. There was a special soda fountain in the game room of the athletes' village, where you could have ice cream dishes made up any way you wanted: toppings and whipped cream, a hundred flavors to choose from. I promised myself I would go there every day when the pairs skating was over. I was always like this. I wasn't able to spoil myself until after a competition. Anna Kondrashova had no such qualms, and every day I jealously watched her eat one of these fabulous sundaes. She let me try a little bite, and it was every bit as good as it looked.

Before the free program, I remember looking at Leonovich, and he was so pale and wan it made me smile. I said to him, "Stanislav Viktorovich, please try to look happy. It can't be as bad as you're making it look with your face." Leonovich always used to get quieter and quieter and quieter before we skated. He never had any last words for us. Even if he'd tried to say something, we never would have heard it, because he'd speak so softly. All the strength went out of him before we competed. The funniest things sometimes popped into my head at such times, and this time I was thinking, Poor Stas, why must he be so nervous for us? He could be home with his wife and kids, completely relaxed and enjoying the skating on television.

We skated the long program as well as we'd ever done it, and by a unanimous vote of the judges, we won the gold medal. Afterward I was proud, but not ecstatic. We didn't organize any special celebration, at least not one in which I was included. Leonovich didn't take me anywhere. Elena and Oleg, who won the silver medal, went out with Sergei, leaving me behind. I was left to enjoy my ice cream by myself, but as it turned out, even that fell through. After waiting all those days, when I went to the game room to create a fabulous sundae, I found they had closed the soda fountain for good. I was so angry that I went to the regular cafeteria and took three bowls of ice cream, but it wasn't the same.

In my journal that night I wrote,

> *I'm in my room, and it's very weird that everything's already over. It all happened so quickly. We were so long preparing for this, then it all happened in one second. Of course I'm very happy. I called my mom from the press center when she was at work at Tass, and she was so surprised. Leonovich told me after the competition that, before the free program, he'd dreamed that we won. He'd never dreamed about figure skating before. He didn't know whether he should tell us about this dream before we skated or not, and didn't know if it was good or bad luck to have this dream. I really want to go home. I really miss my mom. Already, it's a little boring for me here.*

It's mind-boggling that I should have been bored after winning an Olympic gold medal. But understandable, too, since I'd been left behind and had no one with whom I could share my success.

The next day Ryshkin, on behalf of the federation, congratulated us and gave us each $3,860 in cash. I couldn't believe my eyes, because we certainly didn't expect to get any bonus for winning the competition. I was already being paid something like 350 roubles a month salary, which was more than either of my parents were making. But this bonus was more money than I'd ever seen.

The Olympics would continue for another ten days or so, but I can't say that I enjoyed them. Lots of photographers, lots of interviews, very little time with Sergei. I met Peggy Fleming during an ABC interview, and she gave me a red sweater with a panda on the front. *Vogue* magazine wanted to take pictures of me, without Sergei, and they wanted me to wear my skating dress. I didn't like the idea of putting on my skating dress without my skates. Plus they'd made up a set that looked like a forest, and I felt very stupid standing in a skating dress in the forest. I didn't feel comfortable in this picture. I just wanted to be left alone.

What drives me crazy now, when I look back on Calgary, is that I don't remember Sergei from our first Olympics at all. I can't even picture him there, probably because I was so wrapped up in the competition I didn't even look at him. I don't remember if we took a walk together before skating our free program, which we usually did. Or, if we did, where we walked. Or what, if anything, we talked about. I just don't remember, and it makes me angry at myself.

After winning this gold medal, I thought I had to treat myself to something. So I had my hair permed for the first time. I also had my ears pierced and bought some little diamond earrings. Of course I watched all the skating events, and Brian Boitano, Brian Orser, and Viktor Petrenko were just great. And it was fun to watch the showdown between Debi Thomas and Katarina Witt. Debi didn't skate very well. I was sitting right where the "kiss and cry" area was, and her coach, Alex McGowan, was standing there, too. I remember in the middle of her program, Debi turned to him and just said, "Sorry."

Katarina Witt had already skated and had been very good. She was nervously walking around, trying to find a place to stand, stopping here for a little while then running around and stopping there. Always moving, she watched Debi's program. I felt so bad for her because the television camera was right in her face the whole time, recording her reactions. That's probably why she kept moving around, to try to get away from it. I was sitting by myself in the crowd, eating popcorn, and every time the camera panned the audience, it stopped on me. The next day everyone asked me, "How was the popcorn?" It's like Oksana Baiul now. When she goes to hockey games she doesn't know where to sit because the camera always finds her.

The ladies' competition was held the last night of the Olympics, and there I was, alone. I never went anywhere with anyone. All the other athletes were so much older than me, and I must have been the most boring person. I went to one banquet by myself, looking for my friends, but when I peeked in, it was a dark room, and there weren't even chairs set up. Just tables with food, and a refrigerator with drinks and beer. I must have been the first one there, and it looked very scary. So I went back to the dorm.

Someone was standing outside with a bag of fur hats that they wanted to give to all the girls. Because I was the only one they could find, they gave the hats to me. They asked me to pass them out. We were leaving the next day, so I started going around the dorm looking for people, but everyone was out. I had all these hats, and I felt so alone.

For most people, the Olympics were a place to make new friends. Anna Kondrashova, for example, found her husband at the Calgary Games. She fell in love with an athlete from Estonia who competed in Nordic combined. It's why she wasn't in our room very often. Every night she would go out, go walking, so she might meet someone and have a good time. But she was twenty-three.

Sergei, too, made lots of friends at Calgary. But I was too shy. Besides, who would I go make friends with? Hockey players? It's unimaginable. Maybe if I were to have found someone sixteen years old like me, we could have found something fun to do. But I was too timid to even go out of my room, for fear that people would ask me what I was doing or where I was going. I wouldn't have been able to answer them. I enjoyed the actual skating, and was proud of what we accomplished, but it was a long and lonely time for me.

We flew home on a special plane that made four stops along the way and took twenty-one hours. We'd land, get out, go to duty free, buy some more drinks, then load up again. The whole plane went crazy, absolutely crazy. I was probably the only person, including the pilot, who didn't drink anything during the trip. It was February 29, a leap year, and Raisa Smetaniana, the medal-winning cross-country skier, had her birthday on that day, so everyone celebrated the whole way home. We were totally exhausted when we arrived back in Moscow, and a lot of people met us at the airport, bringing us flowers and making speeches.

When I showed my Olympic gold medal to my father, he did the same as he did with all my medals. He put it in a huge glass goblet and filled it with champagne. Then he'd pass this goblet around for everyone to drink from. That's why all the ribbons from my medals are stained.

My father was very proud of me. Once Sergei and I started winning championships, he eased off his criticisms, though he couldn't stop himself from saying something about our costumes every time. "Maybe you shouldn't use this color," he would comment. I didn't take him so seriously anymore. I had my coaches, my choreographer, and my Sergei who would tell me whether something looked good or not. But because my father was an artistic person, he felt he had to say something. He'll always have his opinion, and I've now learned to accept this.

A Time of Change

To celebrate the gold medal, my parents took us to visit Yegor Guba, a friend who raised minks for furriers. He lived on the Volga River, two and a half hours north of Moscow by car, and many Russian figure skaters knew him. He was friendly and generous with his time, and in the summer he would take us swimming and water skiing in the bay of the river. If we wanted to catch fish, he would set out traps for them to swim into—pike and carp, very silvery and shiny, sometimes perch. It wasn't sportfishing. It was like going to the supermarket, because Yegor knew where all the fish lived.

We spent four or five days at Yegor's, snowmobiling, taking saunas, resting, and talking and eating. Sergei came, too, and I at last felt we had celebrated our gold medal together. Then we had to return to Moscow and begin training again for the World Championships, which were held that year in Budapest. It was weird. My feeling was that we had done something so special, and now I was drained emotionally, and I couldn't believe we had to go back on the ice again.

The Olympic year is a very trying period, and most athletes have problems afterward, sometimes for as long as a year or two. It just knocks you off track. I came down with the flu as soon as I got to Budapest, and they were giving me pills and feeding me warm milk. When the time came to skate at the Worlds, I fell on the triple salchow throw during the free program. I couldn't hold the landing. Elena Valova and Oleg Vassiliev took advantage of the mistake and skated very, very well to win for the third time, which was nice for them because it was the last time they were competing before retiring from amateur competition. Elena was so happy, crying and smiling at the same time. She was a very strong-willed person, always having to tape her leg before she skated, always competing in pain. Even though I was upset at my mistake, I could appreciate their joy.

The other thing I remember about that competition was the final girls' practice before the free program. Debi Thomas and Katarina Witt were skating to the same music, *Carmen,* and Katarina, coming off her Olympic triumph, was in unbelievable shape. She felt so relaxed in practice that she brought a camera onto the ice with her and had somebody take her picture in her bodysuit. Then she did something that shocked me.

When Debi started to play her music, Katarina began skating to it. She was doing the movements from her program to Debi's music, and everyone watched only Katarina. The judges, the other skaters, the coaches. Debi didn't know what to do. Katarina had this air about her that said, I'm in the mood to skate right now, and I don't care what anyone thinks. She was doing her triple loop, even though she didn't have it in her program. Of course it's not right to act this way, and I felt sorry for Debi. But this, after all, is sport, and Katarina has a champion's mentality. She knows how to win, and in my opinion, she won the gold medal right there at that practice.

In order to ease the disappointment of losing the World Championships for the first time in three years, I decided to buy myself something nice to wear for the banquet. I don't know what got into me, but I bought a miniskirt, one with a flared hem that was very much in style, and a blouse to match.

I was very, very shy about wearing this outfit to the banquet. But I did it, and I was proud of myself. Sergei saw me and just said "Wow." That helped. I began to understand that in order to get attention, I had to wear something nice, maybe even something a little sexy. Andrei Bukin hung around me all the time at the banquet, and so did Christopher Bowman. Lots of boys did, in fact. Sergei didn't say anything, but it was clear to me that he didn't appreciate it when other boys gave me attention, just as I didn't appreciate it when other girls were around him. If he would go to another girl to talk or to dance—and it was obvious he was popular with the girls—I would also go to another boy.

After the World Championships we went on a twenty-five-city European tour sponsored by the ISU. The European tours were much crazier than the American tours. Anything goes, at least it seemed that way to me. The shows never started on time; the timetables were much more relaxed; and there was never a lot of discipline enforced. After the shows we always had very long dinners, which were often followed by parties, or trips to nightclubs.

I was still much younger than everyone else, and when Sergei went out at night with the older skaters—Marina Klimova and Sergei Pono-marenko, Sasha Fadeev and Liz Manley, Viktor Petrenko—he didn't bring me. They always would go to a bar, and if I were along they'd have had problems getting in. It was upsetting, and made me jealous, but I also understood it. Sergei would say, "Oh Katia, it's okay. Tomorrow we'll sit together on the bus." And he would hug me. Sergei and I grew closer on this tour. He hugged me more often, and would even let me sleep with my head on his shoulder on the bus. That was the best thing for me.

We began to realize that we needed each other off the ice as well as on the ice. Although I still felt insecure about being younger, I saw that I could be interesting to Sergei in the same ways his friends were interesting to him. That we could have conversations about things. That I would take care of him, and he would take care of me.

But it became increasingly painful to be left behind so often. In Europe there were always so many interesting things to see. And whereas before it wouldn't touch me if Sergei would forget to invite me to go for a walk in Paris to see, for example, the Eiffel Tower, or to a park in London, now it began to hurt. "You could have at least asked me," I would tell him. "Maybe I'd like to go, too."

And he'd reply, "Oh, I didn't know. I didn't think of it."

He never took me for walks, just the two of us. So I began going for walks by myself. I was sharing a room with the ice dancer Natalia Bestemianova, and I spent a lot of time with her and her partner, Andrei Bukin, both of whom were married, and with Valova and Vassiliev, who were married to each other. But it felt a little weird. Sergei, meanwhile, was going out with the other skaters who were single. I remember one time on this tour when Sergei was dancing with a German ice dancer. I have a picture of them. It was upsetting, but I never said anything to him about it. He wasn't my boyfriend or someone I could feel I owned. That whole Olympic year was not the happiest one for me.

After the European tour, we had a chance to go on the Tom Collins tour of America. All the other skaters went, but I was so tired of traveling and so homesick that I said no. I told Sergei that I missed my mother and didn't think I'd be able to handle two consecutive tours. It meant, of course, giving up a lot of money, for us and for our coaches. Leonovich talked to me. Tatiana Tarasova talked to me. But I didn't change my mind. Now, looking back, I see that it was probably very stupid. But I can also appreciate it as the first time I had really made a big decision by myself. I hadn't talked to either my mom or dad about it, and certainly Sergei wasn't happy about my decision. But he just told me I had to decide for myself. He didn't try to change my mind.

So while the other skaters flew off to America, Sergei and I went back to Moscow. Life there hadn't changed appreciably for us as a result of our Olympic gold medal. We were a little more recognizable perhaps, but I didn't feel like a celebrity at home. Moscow was so big and busy, and a lot of successful athletes were living there. Our friends still treated us the same. But I got a big surprise when my parents took me on a two-week vacation to the Black Sea. While there, I got a call from our state department inviting me to a dinner that President Mikhail Gorbachev was holding for President Ronald Reagan.

It was exciting, and I just assumed Sergei would be invited too. I thought it would be fun to be there with him, so I rushed back to Moscow, and when I got in I gave Sergei a call. He told me he hadn't been invited to the banquet, but that I should go ahead and attend it alone. I didn't know what I should do. I went, but without Sergei there, or any other friends, I was very bored. I was put at a table with President Reagan, and Raisa Gorbachev was seated beside me. But she didn't talk to me, and I didn't have a very good time.

When I went back to my apartment, I discovered that while I'd been at the Black Sea resort, Sergei had brought me flowers and perfume for my seventeenth birthday. I hadn't told him that I was going to be away. So Sergei had left these gifts with my grandmother, who was almost as excited about them as I was. "Look what Sergei brought you!" She was crazy about Sergei and used to ask me to bring him home for lunch after practice all the time. "Why don't you bring Sergei?" she would say. "I made him his favorite, meatloaf." I sent him a telegram thanking him for the birthday presents. I don't remember why I didn't call him. I think maybe he wasn't home.

I didn't see him for two more weeks, then we met up at a training camp on the Baltic Sea in Jurmala. He looked as if he'd lost weight, and when I looked at him more closely, I saw that he had scars on his arms, with stitches. "What's this?" I asked him, frightened.

He wouldn't tell me. He said, "It's not important for you to know." All I ever learned was that it was some sort of fight. He never talked about such things with me. Or when he was in pain. Or anything bad. It was like he didn't think I should hear about that side of life.

I was growing then, maturing physically. I'd gained a couple of inches in height, so I was now almost five feet two inches tall and weighed ninety-five pounds. My thinking was changing, too, about everything. Absolutely everything. My mom told me it was because of my age, that all girls underwent such changes as their bodies matured, but I still couldn't get used to all these changes and new feelings.

I wrote in my journal that my own nature was driving me crazy. I began being rude to Leonovich, who I now believed wasn't training us hard enough. Sergei would tell me, "Katuuh, he's trying to make us happy in the practice. He's okay." But I wouldn't listen. Because of the changes in my body, I was having trouble landing my jumps. It was like I had to learn everything over again. And then Leonovich would come to the practice and say something like, "Okay, do what you feel like doing this practice. Listen to how your legs are feeling." And I'd get furious, telling Sergei, "He's the coach. He has to tell us what we're supposed to do."

Then I'd get mad at myself for behaving badly to him, and the next day I'd wonder if I was behaving badly or not. Everything I did, I had two opinions about. And I'd try to correct my mood swings. If I was sad, I'd try to make myself happy, which of course I couldn't do.

I didn't have anyone to talk to about these things, except the other half of my Gemini personality. I couldn't talk about it with my sister, who was four years younger than me, or my mother, because I was so often away from home. Or with Anna, who was not that type of friend. So I had no one. I was always keeping my thoughts to myself.

But when I told Sergei about some of my self-doubts, about how I was unsure whether I was too rude to Leonovich for criticizing him for not training us hard enough, Sergei made me very happy by saying he liked me just the way I was.

My heart leaped when he said it, because to me, Sergei was always so much more mature than me, more solid than me, more knowledgeable and sensible. He knew how to get joy from life, how to talk to friends, how to talk to coaches. He knew what he wanted in life. I loved to watch him with his friends, how comfortable he made them feel, how comfortable he was around them. I was even jealous of his friends, because I doubted I could make him feel as happy as they did. I was particularly jealous of Marina, because she could keep Sergei's attention and have long conversations with him. I thought that she had more talent than me, more education, more musical knowledge. With me, Marina only wanted to discuss work and the programs, but with Sergei she talked about other things. It's probably why I became so focused on skating. I assumed they— Marina especially—thought that I was the last person who knew about anything other than skating.

That's why I was so happy when Sergei started to prefer to spend time with me, and talked to me like a friend. Like one of his good friends. When I said something rude to Leonovich in practice, or acted moody, Sergei used to just make a face and say something like, "It's not a good idea what you're doing right now." He never raised his voice. If I kicked the boards with my skate, which he hated, he never yelled. He'd say, "Don't put yourself down. You're not a little kid. If you're disappointed in yourself, don't show it to people. You have to have enough strength to handle it."

I don't know where Sergei got his equanimity from, because his mother was not this way at all. Probably his father had this same mentality. It's why all of Sergei's friends were proud to know him. He was capable of being as wild and crazy as anyone, but when he needed to be strong, he was strong. I saw in Sergei what I was missing in myself, what I was looking for in myself: confidence, stability, maturity. It's why I idolized him so much, why I considered him beyond me and unattainable. He was just a man for my dreams.

Stephan Potopnyk

In Love

I didn't eat properly in the fall of 1988. I suppose I was trying to lose some of the weight I'd put on as my body was maturing. My guess is I wasn't getting enough calcium in my diet, but whatever the reason, I suffered a stress fracture in my right foot, which was diagnosed in November.

My father had driven me to the hospital, and he wouldn't talk to me the whole way home. I was crying, very upset. My foot was already in a cast, and I remember thinking that I shouldn't have said anything about it, that I should have just kept skating with the pain, which was endurable. That's the way my father made me feel. The cast would stay on for a month, then it would be another four weeks before I could get on the ice. It put the entire season in jeopardy, but this time off the ice ended up being a very important period of my life.

If I had been healthy, I wonder if things would have turned out as they did.

I began studying English two days a week with a tutor. I had forgotten everything I'd learned in school, and even had to memorize the letters again. But this was the international language, and I knew it was something I had to do. With my injury, I now had the time. My mother had two grammar books she had saved from when she'd studied English in school, and they helped me a great deal. I had also made a friend in California, a man named Terry Foley, who had sent me a pair of gold earrings after we won the gold medal. He was an engineer with McDonnell Douglas, and during the summer he had come and visited us in Moscow with his three daughters. I wrote him letters a couple of times a month in English, and he would send back my letters with corrections. This, too, helped me to learn.

Sergei either visited or called me every day. Sometimes he came over to dinner, and once I made him a cake. I began to think of myself as someone special in his eyes. My cast came off in mid-December, but the foot was still too painful and weak for skating. Marina told me that ballet exercises were good for rehabilitation, and I went to Navagorsk to work with her on them. I also lifted weights, swam, and practiced lifts with Sergei. He, of course, was also skating and used to run through the new program Marina had created for us by himself.

I went down to the rink to watch him one day in late December. It made my heart ache to have to stand on the side while Sergei skated through our program without me, and silly as it sounds, I worried every day that he might suddenly decide he was not going to wait for me to get healthy and would choose a new partner.

"You look so sad, Katuuh," he said to me, skating over. "So, you'd like to skate?"

"Of course I'm sad. Serioque, you're jumping so well, and when I finally get on skates, I won't be able to jump even two inches off the ice."

He smiled his wonderful, warming smile. "Come on. I'll give you a little ride." And with that he lifted me in his arms and skated me all through our program. It was like flying, and my heart was beating so loudly I was sure he could hear it. It was better than being well.

We invited Sergei to join us again for New Year's, which we were spending this year up at the Volga River home of Yegor Guba. Sergei said he didn't know whether he would come or not. I bought him a bottle of grapefruit liqueur for Christmas. I was so shy, and I thought I'd get him a good bottle of liqueur. It was called Paradise, and came in a green bottle with birds on the label. I found out later this was really the kind of gift you'd give a girl, since it was a sweet liqueur with only 17 percent alcohol. But I didn't know. I was just excited to do it.

On the morning of the thirty-first, my parents

drove to Navagorsk to get me, but Sergei said he was going to celebrate New Year's with Alexander Fadeev instead. So I was quite upset. I wouldn't show him my tears, though, and I gave him my little gift and kissed him on the cheek. I could tell he was happy I did it.

We arrived at Yegor's in the middle of the afternoon, and, still upset, I went up to one of the bedrooms to take a nap. In the meantime Sergei and Sasha had changed their minds. The problem was, they didn't have a car to get to Yegor's, so they had to flag someone down and pay him. On the way they drank the entire bottle of Paradise liqueur.

Sergei came up to my room to wake me. I was so surprised and happy to see him. I think he was a little drunk, because when I asked him about the drive, he said, "Your liqueur was just perfect." Then he asked if I would come with them to see Sasha's property. Fadeev had bought some land nearby, and he'd built a sauna on it. Only a sauna.

I assumed Sergei didn't really want to take a sauna, since Yegor also had one, but was going there to get me away from my parents. The three of us drove to Sasha's land, and Sasha heated up the sauna. In Russia, saunas are usually small log houses that have three rooms. The first room is for taking off the clothes. The next room has benches and a table, because in Russia you must eat and drink, then sauna, then eat and drink some more. The third room has the sauna, which is heated by a wood-burning stove.

Only Sasha took a sauna that day. Sergei and I sat out at the table and talked, and he gave me a small glass of vodka. He said, "I want to tell you something." But whatever it was, he was having trouble saying it. Even the vodka didn't help. I could see he wasn't comfortable, but I knew there was something special on his mind.

Then he said, "Why don't we kiss?" Something like that. It wasn't really a question. He could probably see I wanted it, too. He gave me a gentle kiss on the mouth, and when he saw that I liked it, he gave me another one that was longer. This one was interrupted by Sasha coming out of the sauna to get something to eat. I was so embarrassed I couldn't even look at him.

Sasha must have said something. I don't remember, except I can picture him grabbing something off the table then disappearing back into the sauna by himself. Sergei was smiling. I was probably blushing. Then when Sasha was settled back in the sauna, we kissed a couple times more. This went on for quite a while. Sasha, poor guy, kept staggering out of the sauna to drink vodka and breathe the cool air, embarrassed to interrupt us, but fearful if he didn't he would die of the heat in the sauna. Sergei and I would pretend to be happy to see him, making small talk and biding our time until he plunged back in. Finally at nine o'clock at night Sasha said we'd better get back, since my parents would be wondering where I'd gone. I think he'd lost about ten pounds.

I remember walking back and listening to the cold crunching of the snow beneath our footsteps. The fields were all blanketed in white, and the moon gave us shadows. It was so beautiful, and I was so happy. I wondered, Why me? Why am I so lucky? I was so young and small and shy, and Sergei could have had any nice long-legged girl. Why should he choose me? This is what was going on in my head. I felt much older all of a sudden.

When we got back to Yegor's, all the women went into the sauna. I didn't say anything about being kissed by Sergei. It was my secret, and I didn't want to share it. Maybe because I was worried that Sergei was just in a good mood that day, and that's why he wanted to kiss me. Maybe because, deep down, I believed that he would love me just for a little while, and then it would be over.

Then we got out, dressed for the party, and put on our makeup. I wore the same miniskirt I had worn at the banquet following the World Championships, and I drank champagne at dinner. At midnight, everyone kissed each other as custom demands, but Sergei just kissed me on the cheek, I suppose because my parents were there. We danced and gave gifts to one another, then later shot off the fireworks that Yegor had been saving for the occasion. They showered the snowfields in color.

The next day, Sergei and I had to return to Navagorsk, and we sat together in the back of my parents' car on the way there. We wanted to be alone again as soon as possible, so once we arrived I went with Sergei into his room.

After we had kissed, I asked, "Seriozha, why did you pick me? I'm not old enough. I'm not beautiful enough. My body's not perfect."

But when I had expressed these doubts, Sergei put his fingers to my lips and said, "You're wrong. You're old enough, you're already seventeen. You have a beautiful body. Everything's going to be okay. I love you just the way you are, Katoosha. Just as you are right now."

He was very, very serious. He held me, and I didn't feel the time passing, didn't know what time it was, whether it was day or night. We just hugged and held each other and kissed.

Eventually someone knocked on the door, probably Marina, to find out if Sergei had returned. We stayed quiet and didn't answer. We didn't want anyone to know. I still couldn't believe how fast everything was happening. It had been a year since we first started to feel special things for one another, after Sergei dropped me doing the star lift, and I'd spent six days in the hospital. In all that time, he hadn't kissed me. Thirteen months it had taken us to make that first step. And now, overnight, we were in love.

I didn't tell anyone about these feelings we shared. Not my mother, not my sister, not any of the other skaters. No one at Navagorsk knew about our relationship. Only Sergei's sister, Natalia, knew. Natalia is very, very similar to Sergei. Their smile is the same. Their faces are the same. He had talked to her before that New Year's, saying, "I think I love Katia."

Since it was Sergei who had taken this last step, I was braver with him, more giving, more secure. From this point on, I never paid attention to any other man, not ever again.

On January 9, after almost two months off the ice, I started to skate, but it was not nearly enough time for us to get ready for the European Championships, which were being held that year in Birmingham, England.

Still, the federation sent us to watch the competition. This was in mid-January, and the entire world seemed to have changed in the past two weeks. In the hotel I had my room, and Sergei had his room, but we only used one of them.

It was very important to Sergei that he not scare me. I had no experience at all with men. My mother never really had the chance to tell me about the facts of life. I was just a naive young girl who had no real girlfriends to talk to or ask questions about sex.

I'm sure Sergei didn't expect me to be so inexperienced. But he never rushed me. He cared about my dignity, my modesty, and he was so gentle. He could have said a couple of impatient words, and it would have broken my heart.

Maybe all men are like this, I don't know. He

made some suggestions, and I started to understand that I had to be more sensitive, more tender. He made me feel, suddenly, that I was much older now, that I was a woman. I didn't feel awkward or inadequate, even though I know I was at first. Sergei just couldn't hurt people. He had no meanness in him. None. Every girl, I think, would have loved to have this kind of lover for their first experience with sex.

I don't remember the competition at all. We would take the train from Birmingham to London in the morning and walk around the city. Sergei would go into the pubs and have a beer, and order me a cocktail with my lunch, but I was drunk without drinks. In the evenings we would return to Birmingham to watch the skating, but I was so tired I didn't see anything. Then we'd go back to the hotel and spend another romantic night together, very fun, very wonderful, very little sleep.

We told no one about the change in our relationship. It was so special for me that I didn't want to share it with just anyone. When I finally talked about sex with my mom, and asked her some questions I'd been wondering about, I didn't mention Sergei. Instead, I phrased these questions as if I were curious about my parents: What did you and Daddy do when . . . ? This sort of thing.

She must have known, though. My mom had always loved Sergei. He was more like a friend to her than a son-in-law. He started calling her by her middle name—Levovna—which is very familiar, and which no one else called her, and it made her very happy that he did so. It showed he liked her, and respected her, and that she was a special friend to him. For me, I could never have been so familiar with older people. Sergei's mother, I always called Anna Filipovna. Leonovich, I always called Stanislav Viktorovich. Marina, I always called Marina Olegovna. It was a sign of respect, but it was also a means of keeping some distance. I can't break through this barrier of formality, even now.

Maybe I don't have as much confidence in myself as Sergei did. I'm more reserved. Maybe I don't want to open myself up to closer relationships. I was always jealous of Sergei's ability to be so natural and comfortable with people. He didn't care that they were older. He had read so many books, and some of these books were about people who lived in the villages of rural Russia, where life was not so structured and formal as in the city. And these villagers called each other by their middle names. Sergei took a lot from books. They were very, very important in his life.

He began talking to me for the first time of the things he wanted to do, dreams that he had for the future. Things like the train trip through Europe that he wanted to take me on. I still had not told him "I love you," though he had said these words to me. For me, these were such special words, and I wanted to be sure. You don't just say them casually, and he never asked me to. I was still worried, I think, that for him I was a passing fancy.

After returning to Navagorsk from the European Championships, Marina and I noticed that Sergei was acting sad and pensive, and that he was complaining about things more and more. Sergei never complained, so Marina, who is very direct, asked him what was on his mind. He told her: "I don't want to skate anymore."

This came out of the blue. Marina and I were quite shocked, and we talked to him about it in the dressing room. Sergei said, "I'm twenty-two, and I have nowhere to live. I have to share a room with my parents. I have no car, no apartment, and I spend all my time on the ice. The federation doesn't think of me at all. They promised me a car and maybe an apartment after the Olympics, and they didn't keep their promise. Why, when I'm twenty-two, do I have to live with my mom? I can't spend all my time in Navagorsk."

He was quite serious. Sergei was someone who could have given up skating for good at any time. I didn't feel this dissatisfaction with our life in Navagorsk yet. But I wasn't twenty-two. I thought our life there was wonderful. But Sergei wanted to be able to bring me to his own house without asking his mother's permission or asking his sister to leave. He said he just wanted to have a normal life like other people.

Marina must have talked to someone very high

up, because very soon after that, in February, Sergei got a car. It was a Volga, which is like a Russian tank. And Sergei was also told that very soon he might get an apartment.

Paris

Approaching the 1989 World Championships in Paris, we were more nervous than usual. Because of my foot injury, we hadn't competed all season, and we weren't as prepared as we'd been in other years. In our long program, which was skated to Mozart, I was supposed to be the image of a girl being asked to waltz at her first fancy ball. I was supposed to feel like a young lady for the first time, not a child. This was fitting for my own life, too, but Sergei and I tried to skate the same as we always did; and truthfully, it felt no different to skate with him now than before we were in love. The big change had been after he dropped me on the ice a year earlier. Since then, Sergei had always held me like I was something he was afraid to lose.

We wanted Marina to accompany us to Paris. Up until that time, only the coaches traveled with Russian skaters, never the choreographers. But because she had helped me so much with my rehabilitation, overseeing my ballet exercises, and because she had spent so much time with us both on and off the ice that year, we wanted Marina to be with us for the Worlds. We talked to Leonovich about it, and he said we had to go to the federation and ask them. He told me it was important that I say something to them myself at this meeting. So Sergei, Leonovich, and I did this, which was quite unusual, and would have been impossible for anyone but the Olympic champions. At the meeting I told Alexander Gorshkov, who was the head of the federation, how great it would be for me if Marina were there. So they agreed to send her.

When I think about this time in Paris, I just want to smile and smile. It was the first and only time in my career that the competition meant nothing to me. Nothing. It was warm and sunny outside, I was in love, and I remember warming up on the fresh green grass wondering why in such a gorgeous city with such beautiful weather did we have to go into an ice rink and compete? We could just be walking and walking. I only wanted to get our programs over with. I can't say I didn't care if we won or lost, but I didn't worry and concentrate the way I had always done.

It didn't seem to hurt our performance. We didn't miss anything, although we had taken out one of our double axels, so it wasn't as difficult a program technically as we'd skated in the past. But we won, and for winning they gave us seven thousand French francs each.

To celebrate, Sergei took me to lunch at a restaurant. He was drinking beer, and he ordered me a cocktail, which I didn't like. Then the manager recognized us and brought us a bottle of champagne. I was drinking it very fast, and I got so drunk. It was delicious, actually. We had tried not to tell people that we were now boyfriend and girlfriend, but the other skaters realized that I had grown up, and that I now had more of a woman's body. And after this lunch we were laughing and kissing on the street. I didn't care if anyone saw us. We didn't take a taxi back to the hotel. We just walked, and sat on the park benches, and watched the people and watched each other. The atmosphere in Paris will make you feel special even if you're not in love. And for me, this day could have lasted forever.

Then Sergei said we had to invite Marina and Alexander Fadeev to a restaurant, too. So the day after Sasha finished the singles, we said we would meet them at a restaurant on the Champs-Elysées.

The time came, and Sergei and I were still back in our room. Who cares? So we're late? I was just drunk all the time with love. Marina and Sasha called our room to find out what was the matter. "Oh, we're coming," I said. "Don't worry." When we arrived, Marina looked at us like, What's going on with you two? That, I think, was the first time she knew there was something between us.

Sergei had bought flowers for me, and flowers for Marina. She was quite upset at first because she had left Vasily, her stuffed animal that brought us good luck, in the taxi that had brought her to the restaurant. Vasily was a hedgehog that had originally belonged to me. Marina came to my room one time and saw all the pink animals, yellow ones, green ones, blue ones, white ones, and purple ones—and this one poor gray hedgehog. He looked very plain, and Marina said, "I feel very sorry for this toy."

I said to her, "If you're sorry, Marina, take him with you and give him a better life." Which she did. He saw the world. But now she had left him in a taxi in Paris.

It was a seafood restaurant, and we asked the waiter to bring us a little of everything for the first course. He delivered this huge tray of ice covered with shellfish: mussels, oysters, shrimp, clams, scallops, crab legs, periwinkles. I didn't think I'd have the courage to even try these things. I didn't know it was possible to eat them. But they were delicious, and we laughed as we watched each other try to get them out of their shells. I saw people at the other tables eating their oysters so professionally, and couldn't figure out how they were doing it. It was very impressive.

Then Sergei said, let's call home. So we did, and I was so surprised to be talking to my parents from a pay phone in a restaurant in Paris.

We kept ordering more shellfish and bread. Loaves and loaves of bread. It took us five hours to eat, and we never had a main course. It was all appetizers, and three bottles of Chablis, which was the first time I'd ever had it. The people at the tables around us changed many times, we were there for so long. And at the end Sergei insisted on paying for everything.

Afterward we went back to the hotel by taxi, and who do you think was sitting in the back of this cab? Vasily. Marina said he was indeed a very lucky hedgehog, and that he had showed us his power that day. Back at the hotel, Sergei kept buying drinks at the bar, and he bought me a Bloody Mary. But I didn't drink it. I was drunk enough from Paris and the wine.

The next day we visited Notre Dame cathedral. It was strange, but I'd always been afraid of churches. During the European tour in 1988, we stopped several times to visit the famous cathedrals: in Milan, in Prague. But I didn't feel comfortable there. I knew what God was, but I was a little scared because my family had never gone to church. Both my grandfather and father were army men, and this was the period of time in the Soviet Union when it was illegal to believe in God. You couldn't speak about religion at home or in school. Either of them could have been demoted if it had been discovered we were worshiping at home.

I do remember both my grandmothers praying, however. Babushka kept an icon on the wall at home. And my other grandmother, my father's mother, who lived in another apartment in

Moscow, had an icon that she kept behind a curtain so people wouldn't see it when they walked in. She would light a little candle, the kind that is just a wick floating in oil, and would pray to this icon every night. I had never seen this done before, and when I was visiting her one time, I asked what she was doing. She told me she was praying, and said that when I got older, I'd pray, too. So when I was young I thought that only grandmothers prayed.

In the cathedrals, though, the smell of the incense made me feel sick to my stomach. I thought that death smelled this way. Sergei was the one who took me to a church for the first time in Milan, saying, "You definitely have to see this, Katuuh, because you may never be back again." He was interested, not because he was religious, but because the cathedral was so beautiful. He told me it was okay. "Don't be frightened," he said. "I'll hold your hand." Then he explained it was not a cemetery. That it was incense I smelled, not death. "It's a beautiful building," he said. "It's history."

He took me inside, and with him holding my hand, all these stupid fears went away.

So I was no longer frightened when, in Paris, we went to the cathedral of Notre Dame, and afterward we sat on the steps out front and watched the people. It is a wonderful place to people watch, the steps of Notre Dame. Walking through the city, through Paris, in spring, being in love—what else could you wish for in life? It was here that I first said "I love you" to Sergei.

We thought we'd come back sometime and spend ten days there at least, just walking around Paris when the weather was nice. It was one of our dreams. But of course we never did.

Romeo, Juliet, and a Froggy Village

Afterward we were invited to do the European tour, and Sergei and I were too shy to ask for our own room. My roommate was Elena Bechke, another pairs skater from Russia, and so many times she would try to get in, but the door would be locked, and it was very embarrassing for everyone. Everyone now knew that Sergei and I had a relationship.

It was still important for me to skate well, and because my body had changed, and the European rinks were cold, and we had very little opportunity to warm up, I often made mistakes. I'd get upset, as usual, and would put on a big frown. Sergei would try to cheer me up: "Don't be upset, Katuuh, we have another show tomorrow." But sometimes he just gave up.

Other people, however, would misunderstand.

"Katia, is everything all right?" the other skaters would ask when they saw my face. They assumed this expression could only have been caused if something was wrong between me and Sergei. I didn't like it when people asked me these things.

I sometimes would be sad the whole next day, not smiling, not speaking, because I missed a jump. I'd be wondering, Am I not working hard enough? Should I be spending less time touring and more time at the gym? Should I only practice my jumps? What will happen next fall? Sometimes I couldn't even explain to Sergei all the different worries that were in my head. It wasn't for another year that he figured out there was nothing he could say to make me feel better if I was not skating well. I never learned to leave my skating on the ice, where it belonged. The only thing he could do was take my hand. This never changed. Just by touching me Sergei could fix a problem.

He started to suggest books for me to read. *Gone With the Wind* was one, and I liked it very much. But I had no memory for books. If I read a book, I'd forget what it was about tomorrow; and the day after tomorrow, I'd have forgotten I ever read it in the first place. I don't know what I think about when I read. But Sergei remembered everything. He hungered for information. Sergei's favorite authors were Boris Pasternak—he read *Doctor Zhivago* three times—Chekhov, and Mikhail Bulgakov, who wrote his favorite book, *Master and*

Margarita. He could have read this book year after year.

Marina used to take us to museums, and she'd be explaining some painting to us, when out of the blue Sergei would say something that showed he already knew very well the meaning of the painting. I don't know where he found the time to read so much. He'd rather read a book than watch a movie, or play golf, or almost anything, and if you tried to interrupt him, it was as if he were suddenly deaf and you were invisible.

Sergei was also crazy about dogs. He could talk about dogs all day long, and so could Marina. Once the three of us drove from Megeve, where we trained, to Paris—a six-hour drive—and the whole way he and Marina talked about dogs. So that spring, after the tour, he got a bull-terrier puppy that he named Moshka. It was white, with a black ring around its left eye. He picked it out with my mother, and they brought it home in a basket.

In mid-May Sergei, Moshka, and I went to our dacha for ten days, just the three of us. This was now a new dacha, which I had helped my parents purchase in the village of Ligooshina, which means "froggy village," even though I never saw any frogs. The apple trees were in blossom, the grass was green, and everything was fresh with spring. We did nothing in those ten days, no training, no jogging. We just relaxed and played with the dog. Almost every evening we made a fire to

cook on, and I'd make Sergei a shish kebab.
When the fire had burned down to coals, we'd
throw potatoes into the coals to bake them, completely unwrapped. When they were cooked
Sergei would peel them for me, because they were
too hot for my hands to hold.

Moshka

It was the first time Sergei and I had ever spent
so much time alone together. I didn't see any different sides to him than those I already knew. He
was calm and happy, never moody. He loved to
play with his dog, and would carefully cut fresh
meat for Moshka every day, which we'd cook
very quickly by pouring boiling water over it.
There was no dog food in Ligooshina. I cooked
for Sergei, big breakfasts and creative dinners:

sausages, chicken, meat, eggs. He liked whatever I made him. My grandmother had taught me to cook.

My favorite thing, then and always, was to drive with Sergei in the car. This was our chance to be alone. Before he got his apartment, we used to laugh that we would probably live in a car some-day, set up house there and raise our children. A little stove in the glove compartment. I'd put my head on his shoulder as he drove, and Sergei would listen to music—Bon Jovi, Annie Lennox. The last couple of years he'd started listening to Russian rock groups, too, because he liked the lyrics. He'd drive until he found a nice place to stop, then we'd talk or kiss. He gave me cognac sometimes so I'd relax. He told me the first time, "Try it, Katoosha. It's very nice." And he was right.

I still like the taste of cognac. It doesn't make you crazy, it just warms you from the inside out, like a cozy fire. It remains burned in my memory that it was always exciting to be in a car with Sergei, when it was dark outside and he was dri-ving.

❊   ❊   ❊

Marina chose *Romeo and Juliet* for us to skate to in the 1989/90 season. There were two variations that we listened to, one by Prokofiev and one by Tchaikovsky, and she asked us which one we pre-ferred. It was the first time she'd ever given us a chance to choose, and we liked the Tchaikovsky variation right away, because it sounded more danceable. I was excited about the program, and went to the *Romeo and Juliet* ballet to get some ideas. Marina got Vladislav Kostin from the Bolshoi Ballet to do our costumes. The whole process of creating this program felt different.

We decided to do our elements—the throws, the lifts, the spirals—in a different order than usual. We thought we should listen to the music and decide what elements fit the music, rather than do the death spiral at the end, for example, because that's when death spirals are done. And we were surprised to discover that it was easier to skate that way.

Sergei was never the first to suggest something. He'd be standing over by the boards, quiet, so quiet, while Marina, Leonovich, and I would be trying to put a certain element into a particular part of the program, maybe our side-by-side double axels. Then Sergei would simply say this element doesn't go there. And he'd be right. Working on this *Romeo and Juliet* program was the first time that Marina began to trust, even depend on, Sergei's judgment. He wouldn't even try to do an element in a section if he knew it didn't fit. He wasn't going to break himself in half trying to learn something that he intuitively knew didn't feel right. If he liked it, though, he said so immediately.

I felt like we had reached the next level in our skating. Marina sensed it, too. She had seen us walking hand in hand together in the street, whereas before we would never touch each other in public. It gave her more range and flexibility in creating her programs. We could touch each other in new ways on the ice, even kiss each other.

Training camp in the summer of 1989 was first in Georgia, in Sukhumi, and then in a ski resort in the mountains called Terskul. I remember Terskul very well because of a scary thing that happened to me there. I was in a room by myself, with Sergei in a room next door. We never stayed the night together when we were training.

In the middle of the night I heard a banging at my balcony window. For some reason I had left my light on, and I sleepily opened the balcony door to find two men in their thirties, complete strangers, standing there. They explained that they had locked themselves out of the hotel, and because mine was the only light still shining, they'd climbed up to see if I would let them into the hotel. I don't know how they did this, since I was on the fifth floor. I didn't even think it might be dangerous.

Both the men were very drunk, but one was drunker than the other, and this man grabbed me from behind. I was so scared that I tried to scream but couldn't. This was the first time I ever learned about being so frightened that you cannot make a sound. I tried to hit him with my elbow, and with my foot tried to kick against the wall to Sergei's room. But I couldn't do it. Thank

God the other man came back and told his friend to let me go. Then he led him away.

Surprisingly, they came back a short time later. They knocked on my door, and I again opened it for them. I must have been very sleepyheaded. When I realized my mistake, I tried to slam it shut again, but they didn't let me. Again, thank God there were two of them, because the one who was not so drunk said, "Come on, let's go. People will hear us." And he pulled the drunk one away from the door. They came back a third time, too, but this time I left the door locked. I was so embarrassed about the whole incident that I didn't tell anyone this story the next day, and only mentioned it to Sergei years later.

That fall Sergei's dog, Moshka, died. We had been at an exhibition in Germany, and Sergei's mother, Anna, was taking care of the dog. It stopped eating one day, and she didn't do anything about it at first. When Sergei came home, he took Moshka to the vet right away. It had been four days since she had eaten. Sergei had not given Moshka her puppy shots, and she was suffering from distemper. The vet gave her these shots, but by then it was too late. Sergei took Moshka home, and that night the puppy pushed open his bedroom door, which she had never done before, and Sergei lifted her into his bed. Two hours later she died.

Sergei called me in the morning and told me. It was very, very sad for him. He buried her near his home, in the forest, and didn't skate that day. He later said to me, "Why do things happen to the ones I love?" And that was the first time he told me that his best friend had died a few years earlier in a car crash. It was the younger brother of Viacheslav Fetisov, the famous Red Army hockey player, who later came to America and played in the National Hockey League. A short while later I gave Sergei a porcelain figure of a white bullterrier with a black left eye, just like Moshka, which he always kept, and I have still.

*   *   *

Sergei's shoulder started bothering him that year. Leonovich had taught us a new lift that we called a loop lift, in which my feet were positioned as if I were doing a loop jump, my hand was behind my back, and Sergei took this hand and lifted me up with one arm as I split my legs. I never saw anyone else doing this lift, but it was the move that hurt Sergei's shoulder — although we didn't realize it for a long time. It bothered him enough that we had to drop out of the Nationals, missing them for the second year in a row.

He didn't complain, but I knew he was in a lot of pain. The doctors at the Central Army Hospital said there was nothing they could do except give him shots to ease his discomfort. They thought there was some problem with his muscles, but they really had no idea how to cure it, and it was a year later that a doctor in the United States figured out that he had torn his rotator cuff.

For New Year's 1990, we again returned to celebrate with Yegor. So much had happened in the
last twelve months, so much within me had
changed, I could hardly believe it was just a year
ago that Sergei had kissed me for the first time.
Now, of course, as I write this, I'd give anything to
go back and relive 1989. Every moment of it, good
and bad, starting with the trip to Sasha Fadeev's
sauna, then to Birmingham, to Navagorsk, to
Paris, to the dacha in Ligooshina, even to Terskul,
with the drunks on the balcony. I'd go back there
in a heartbeat, and remain.

But I held no such nostalgic notions at the time.
It seemed as if the happiest years with Sergei were
just beginning, that the best times were in the
future, not the past. Nineteen ninety was just one
more New Year's Eve at Yegor's. I had no desire to
drag Sergei back to Fadeev's sauna, to relive our
special kiss. I could kiss him anywhere I liked
now—anytime, with anyone watching. We danced
a lot. We drank champagne. We watched the fireworks. In Russia, each New Year has a special
color, and I remember that in 1990 the color was
white. Sergei wore a white sweater I had knitted
him, and as always, he looked very, very handsome. My parents, again, were there; my sister,
Maria; Sasha; and lots of Yegor's friends. People
from his village used to drop by his home to celebrate every New Year, because everyone knew
Yegor, everyone liked him, and this tradition
brought all the people luck.

The European Championships that year were in Leningrad, and we weren't in very good shape. Sergei's shoulder was only part of the problem. I was still having difficulty with my jumps, because of my body change. In the short program at Leningrad we were atrocious. I missed the double axel and slipped doing the death spiral. Also one of our spins was not in sync. The next morning we heard on television that the Moscow pairs team of Gordeeva and Grinkov was very bad and probably could not win the gold medal. It motivated us, and the day of the free program Marina told me, "Ekaterina Gordeeva, you're the Olympic champion, remember?"

It helped me. Those were the only words I remember a coach saying to me before I skated that actually helped me. I still think of those words sometimes before I take the ice. In the long program, we skated *Romeo and Juliet* very cleanly, and everyone loved it, and we came back from third place to win. This program, which Marina had created to reflect the feelings we were having for each other off the ice, was a big plus for us all year. I felt like I understood the reason behind every movement I made. But even though Sergei skated this program so tenderly, and looked at me always so lovingly, we were all business on the ice. We never complimented each other after we skated. He never whispered in my ear, "I love you." That was for later, when we were off the ice. Though to be honest, Sergei was never much of

Gerard Vandystadt/Allsport

1990 World Championships

one for compliments or flattery. He never said I looked beautiful, or fresh, if I tried to look especially nice for him. The most he ever said was "Wow," although he said other things with his eyes.

We didn't skate our best at the 1990 World Championships, either, which were held in Halifax. Again, we won, but I two-footed my triple toe jump and fell on the double axel. Afterward Sergei said to Marina, "What if I missed a jump? Can you believe how bad I would look? Katia's little, she's tiny, she's a girl. But if I missed, what do you think would happen?" He dreaded this thought. He was all the time worried about me, and I never, ever worried about him.

❖   ❖   ❖

We again went on the Tom Collins tour that spring. Financially, the way it worked was that Tom would give all the skaters money for the first third of the tour, then the next third, then the last third. The skaters from the Soviet Union, however, were not allowed to open their envelopes until the head of the Soviet skating federation, Alexander Gorshkov, came to pick them up. Then he'd give us some money back. I never knew if the money we were getting back was one-quarter of what Tom paid us or one-half. We were always upset it wasn't more, because we saw that skaters from the other countries got to keep all the money that they were paid. Eventually we started to complain as a group, led by our coaches, and Gorshkov began giving us a little bit more. We still spent everything we earned.

The Russians on these tours always liked to have room parties together. The boys would buy the liquor, and the girls would buy the food—salami, peanuts, gherkin pickles—which we washed down with a shot of vodka. We didn't have so much money that we could order room service.

This particular time I roomed with Galina Zmievskaya, who was Viktor Petrenko's coach. She always had smoked meat, salami, sausages, and a huge chunk of chocolate that she carried

Time off during our 1990 Tom Collins tour.

along for meals. We saved money this way. It's why I always brought along a hot water kettle for making coffee and tea. Galina made Viktor, Sergei, and me feel like she was the mom taking care of us. In the morning she'd wake up and say to me, "Let's call our boys and ask them for breakfast." Then she'd call Viktor and Sergei, who were also rooming together, and would break out her food.

Viktor was always very quiet around me, but friendly, and absolutely dependable as a friend. I respect him even more as a person than I do as a skater. Any favor you asked of him, he'd say it was no problem. He told Sergei that if he ever wanted to have the room to himself, he'd be happy to move somewhere else for the night. But we never asked him to do this.

Viktor worked very hard with Galina, and I was amazed how much time they spent together, both on and off the ice. I didn't realize it then, but Viktor was already engaged to Galina's daughter, Nina. He and Galina would go to restaurants together, go walking together, everything. He never went out at night with the other men. And Galina wouldn't let him play basketball or soccer, which all the other skaters did, for fear he would hurt himself. I thought it was all too much. But I never heard Viktor complain about it.

When the tour got to Washington, D.C., we were staying at the Four Seasons Hotel when Viktor called me very late one night. He asked me if I could come to his room right away. He had something important to tell me. When I got there, Viktor said that Sergei had just gotten a call from Leonovich. Sergei's father had died of a heart attack. Sergei had put his clothes on and gone out, Viktor didn't know where. He thought we should go look for him.

We started checking the bars in the area, but we couldn't find him. Finally we returned to the hotel and found Sergei sitting at the bar. He couldn't talk about his father then, and I didn't know what to say. I just hugged him. I just tried to hold him all the time. It was the first time I'd ever had a close friend have someone in his family die, and I felt so terrible because I didn't know what to talk to him about.

Sergei was crying, and he told me, "I didn't spend enough time with my father."

I, too, wished I had spent more time with him. I still feel this way, because I only met him two times, and his father was the one whom Sergei resembled, on the inside and the outside. He was so big and so solid.

The next morning Sergei flew back to Moscow on the first flight he could get. He didn't want me to come, but I drove him to the airport. I later learned that my mother was a big help finding a cemetery plot for Sergei's father. These plots were in very short supply in Moscow, but my mother offered Anna a place in the plot of her own family.

Sergei came back to the tour shortly after the

funeral. He was exhausted and looked as if he had lost weight. I bought him flowers and champagne. He brought me a bottle of cognac. I was so happy to see him, but he was too filled with grief to be happy.

He said to me, "Every year, it's something. First my best friend. Then Moshka. Then my father." He was also very concerned about his mother, Anna, because she was inconsolable when he'd been back in Moscow. His father, who'd had three heart attacks earlier in his life, had collapsed in Anna's arms. She had held him as he took his last breath. It was just the two of them at their dacha, which he had built with his own hands, and there was no phone and no one nearby to come to help her. So it was very hard on Sergei's mom.

I asked Sergei to tell me stories about his father. He said he was just a quiet man who liked to be alone, and who was a high-ranking officer in the police. It wasn't much to be left with. Sergei had never spent very much time with his father, since he had never been involved in Sergei's skating. It was his mother who oversaw all that. Sergei, I knew, would be much more involved in the lives of his own children. Some men are natural fathers, even before they are fathers, and Sergei was this kind of man.

Some Proposals

*I*n May, just prior to my nineteenth birthday, I was baptized. My mom had become good friends with a neighbor who was very religious, and they decided that since the churches were reopening in the Soviet Union, it was time I should be christened in the Russian Orthodox faith. When my mother was four years old, she told me, her grandmother had secretly had her baptized. She further explained that if I wasn't christened, it would be impossible for me to be married in a church. "Katia," she asked, "don't you want to be married in church?"

I told her I did, although no one had yet spoken to me of marriage. I'd started to like churches since Sergei had taken me by the hand into the stunning cathedrals of Milan and Paris. I loved the way the music sounded as it echoed off the stone walls. I thought a church would be a beautiful place in which to be married.

This friend of my mother's said she knew a very good priest, and she introduced me to this priest when he was visiting her family one day. His name was Father Nikolai, and I immediately liked this man. He had a very kind face. He was forty-five or

Father Nikolai

fifty years old, and had long, straight black hair, which was always brushed carefully. His beard was also long and had streaks of gray in it. His eyes were very gentle, and he spoke in a soft and soothing voice.

I didn't know anything about religion. I didn't even know how to cross myself, but Father Nikolai never made me feel shy about it. He just told me he would give me some prayers to learn, or if I didn't have time to learn them by heart, I could read them. He didn't preach to me about doing this and this and this. He simply told me I could always come talk to him if I felt the need to. He made it sound as if he would be the guardian of my spirit, and he has turned out to be just that.

Father Nikolai's church was called the Church of Vladimir the Conqueror. Churches in Russia are always named after the oldest icon in the church's collection, and this icon of Vladimir the Conqueror shows him riding a horse and carrying a spear. It is a warlike pose, and he does not appear to be a very holy figure. But he is probably poised to drive off the barbarian infidels and save many defenseless Russian churches, which is why, many years ago, they created this icon of him. Father Nikolai asked if I wished to be christened in the Church of Vladimir the Conqueror by myself or with other people, and I said I preferred to do it alone.

They had just finished adding a small church to the courtyard beside the big church, and this was where the service took place. Everything was new and beautiful, and I was the first person christened in this little chapel. In Russia, you are baptized while wearing only a nightshirt, so Father Nikolai told me to bring a white nightshirt and my own cross. He would bless my cross by immersing it in the holy water. Then he would splash this water all over me. The water was supposed to be cold, but the lady who was helping Father Nikolai took pity on me and brought in warm water so I wouldn't freeze. It was very private: just Father Nikolai, this lady, and me. I had asked my parents and Sergei not to come. It seemed to me that such a moment should be a personal affair.

Afterward, I didn't feel particularly different, but I did feel the baptism was something special and a little exciting. Something had changed, even if I couldn't explain what.

* * *

Almost every other weekend in the summer, Sergei and I went to visit Yegor at his house on the Volga River. It was beautiful there. Sergei thought this was the best vacation you could have: fishing, walking in the forest, being outside, making dinner from the fish that you caught. I agreed with him.

Then it was time for the usual visits to training camps: Sukhumi and Navagorsk in preparation for the Goodwill Games that were being held in Seattle. Sergei's shoulder was still bothering him, and while we skated well in practice, during the actual Goodwill competition we were terrible. I fell doing a double axel and again two-footed my triple toe. It was quite upsetting, and I began talking to Sergei about the possibility of changing coaches. We just hadn't skated that well the year before, despite winning, and I wanted someone who would push us a little harder. Since I was the one making the mistakes on the ice, I was the one who wanted the change. But Sergei was starting to agree with me.

The Goodwill Games was also the place where we met Jay Ogden from the International Management Group (IMG) for the first time. Paul Theofanous, who spoke Russian and also worked for IMG, introduced us. Paul was a Greek from New Jersey, but his Russian was very good, and Sergei and I liked him.

He and Jay met with us for half an hour, explaining that IMG managed the careers of professional athletes. They owned and produced the North American show Stars on Ice, and told us they could give us a contract if we agreed to turn professional. They told us we could definitely earn more than a hundred thousand dollars a year, maybe much more, if we signed to skate in the show the next season, and if we also competed in some professional competitions. But we didn't take them very seriously. It seemed more like they were trying to own us than help us. So we didn't sign anything then.

Besides, Sergei and I still wanted to skate in the World Championships, and maybe another Olympics, and if we turned pro we'd lose our ISU eligibility. The ISU allowed skaters to be paid a small salary during tours that they sanctioned, such as the Tom Collins tour, but it was a very specific amount, something like five hundred Swiss francs a month. It varied year to year. As a professional, you could earn fifty times that amount, but those additional earnings came with a price. The biggest competitions in skating—the World Championships, the Europeans, and the Olympics—were only open to amateurs.

We had a couple of exhibitions in Sun Valley after the Goodwill Games, then I went to visit my friend Terry Foley in California. He had invited my sister, Maria, and mother to stay with him, and it was the first time they'd ever been to the United States. I felt I should go, too. Sergei wasn't very happy about it, though. He didn't know what to make of Terry. He was a little suspicious of his motives, even though Terry's oldest daughter was older than me. So Sergei went back to Moscow on his own, and I ended up being a rude houseguest who was always in a terrible mood, because I thought I should be back in Moscow with Sergei.

That entire fall, and most of the winter and the following spring, was one of the most stressful periods of our lives. There was still the matter of changing coaches to deal with, and when I got back to Moscow, Sergei and I talked to the skating federation about this idea. Did they have any suggestions? Maybe Tatiana Tarasova, someone said. She had coached the famous pairs team of Irina Rodnina and Alexander Zaitsev, who'd won

Here I am, long before I put
on my first pair of skates.

One of my favorite pictures of
Sergei as a young boy.

Veld, our beloved Great Dane.

At Calgary, we skated our free program as well as
we'd ever done it.

Our off-ice training included other sports like skiing. Here we are
in 1989 in Terskul with *(left to right)* a trainer; our choreographer
Marina Zueva, our coach Stanislav Leonovich.

Richard Mackson/Sports Illustrated
After winning the gold medal at the 1988 Olympics.

This photo was taken with family members before
our wedding in 1991. *Left to right:* Sergei's sister, Natalia,
Sergei's mother, my father and mother.

Our church wedding on April 28, 1991
was performed by Father Nikolai.

Soon after our wedding we went on tour to South Africa.
Here we are on safari, playing with some lion cubs.

Newlyweds, and very much in love.

The year we were married was
the first time we toured with
Stars on Ice.

While I was pregnant with
Daria, Sergei took care of me
so tenderly.

Sergei and I had such fun
watching Daria grow up.

Sergei adored Daria and was a wonderful father.

Whenever possible, we tried to bring my mom and Daria along with us when we were on tour.

Georges De Keerle/Sygma
Reunited with Daria in Moscow, 1994.

Clive Brunskill/Allsport

This gold medal we won for each other.

Heinz Kluetmeier

"It's almost like you were preparing your whole career for this program," said Marina Zueva, who created our *Moonlight* Sonata program for the 1994 Lillehammer Olympics.

Left to right: My sister, Maria, with our dear friends Yegor Guba and Debbie Nast.

Sergei with his friends *(left to right)* Alexander Zhulin and Artur Dmitriev on tour with Tom Collins in 1994.

Taking time out from practice at Simsbury with *(left to right)* Marina Zueva, Daria, Marina's son Fedor, and my mom.

With Kitty and Peter Carruthers in Aspen during our first year with Stars on Ice.

Sergei preparing to jet ski with Paul Wylie and Denis Petrov.

Sergei always knew how to enjoy himself with friends. Here he is with *(left to right)* Genrikh Sretenski, Rosalynn Sumners, and Denis Petrov.

Fooling around with Stars on Ice friends in Lake Placid only days before Sergei's death. *Left to right:* me, Scott Hamilton, Kristi Yamaguchi, a friend of Rosalynn Sumners's, Sergei, Christine Hough, and Rosalynn Sumners.

Skating Together:

Dino Ricci

Marina created the Rodin number for us in 1994, based on the poses in Rodin's sculptures. It was my favorite exhibition piece.

In December 1994, we won the World Professional Championships for the third time, skating a Gershwin program as our technical number.

Irene Ersek

Paul Reid

"The Man I Love" skated during our Stars on Ice tour 1994/95.

Many Competitions, Many Memories

Irene Ersek

We added our "Porgy and Bess" program shortly after the 1994 Olympics.

Irene Ersek

"Out of Tears" skated to the Rolling Stones was one of our numbers in the 1994/95 Stars of Ice tour.

In Summer 1995, we were working on this new program, but never got a chance to skate it.

Heinz Kluetmeier

"Celebration of a Life"
February 27, 1996

Heinz Kluetmeier

Daria and me with all our wonderful friends
who came together to celebrate Sergei's life.

As I skated to Mahler's
Symphony No. 5, I sensed
Sergei's presence in
my heart, my soul,
everywhere.

Far right:
By the time the
tribute reached its finale,
I felt relaxed and
happy, even joyful.

Heinz Kluetmeier

One of the last
photographs taken of
the three of us,
November 1995.

Yuri Dojc

Christopher Little

With Daria, 1996. She is always smiling for me.

two Olympic gold medals and six World Championships, before she coached ice dancers Bestemianova and Bukin.

My father, in fact, was working for Tatiana Tarasova. She ran the Russian All-Stars skating tour that gave exhibitions throughout the world, and my father was helping with the costumes. He started lobbying Sergei and me about joining the All-Stars and having Tarasova coach us. Of course we wanted Marina to come with us, too. So when we agreed to have an interview with Tarasova, Sergei called Marina to ask her to come along. But Marina wouldn't do it. She told him she couldn't work with Tarasova. They were very different people. Both were choreographers, but they each had their own vision about what skating should be. This meant we'd have to leave Marina, as well as Leonovich, if we went with Tarasova, which we eventually did.

Then Paul Theofanous came to Moscow to visit us, and it was during this trip that we agreed to sign a contract with IMG. That, in itself, didn't mean we had decided to turn professional. There were no numbers on this contract. IMG wasn't paying us anything, and we weren't agreeing to skate in Stars on Ice. But the contract said IMG would represent us for the next two years and could use our name to promote any events we were skating in.

Sergei and I made this decision together without telling anyone else. We started to work with

Tatiana on our new programs for the 1991 season, but Sergei's shoulder was giving him a lot of pain, and all we could practice were spirals, steps, and spins. No throws. No lifts. We didn't feel we were growing as skaters. Sergei, especially, felt this. We were stale, unmotivated. He said if we stayed amateur two more years, he wouldn't want to skate at all afterward. We'd totally burn out. He said to me, "Let's turn pro before we get so sick of the ice we can't look at it."

We decided to talk to Tatiana about it. She's a big woman, full of energy and with an endless stream of ideas. She is also a chain-smoker with a thermos of pills in her bag for every conceivable ailment. But she was just the person we needed at that point in our careers, always smiling and enthusiastic, very concerned about our health. We liked working with her.

Tatiana didn't try to talk us into turning pro, or out of turning pro. She did say, however, that if we decided to skate professionally, she would call Dick Button in New York and tell him that we'd like to compete in the World Professional Championships in Landover, Maryland, in December. You could tell she thought it was a wonderful idea. She also said that if we joined her Russian All-Stars, whose schedule conflicted with Stars on Ice, she would pay us a salary of four thousand dollars a week, every week, even when we were training. That turned out to be a wildly inflated number, but Jayne Torvill and Christopher Dean had just left the All-Stars, and Tatiana was desperate to have some big-name skaters join her. That's when we told her we had already signed with IMG, which surprised her.

Sergei and I thought about it for a day, then decided to give up amateur skating. Tatiana said, "Great! I'll call Dick Button! We must start work today on your program." Sergei and I never regretted our decision for a minute.

My father, however, was so disappointed. Here he had finally gotten us to go to a coach he approved of, and we were turning professional. No 1992 Olympics. No Europeans. No Soviet national competitions. My father was like, "Oh my God, what have I done!" He blamed it on Tatiana, mistakenly believing it was all her idea.

Tatiana had us working on new moves every day, and very quickly we had three programs to use in Landover in December. Professional skating is quite different from amateur skating—less technical, more theatrical—and I think she is a better coach for professionals than for amateurs. She likes creating dramatic programs rather than drilling her skaters repeatedly on double axels and lifts and other required elements. I liked working with her. She had a real talent for talking to people, and was great with Sergei. She really made him work. He might say, "That's enough for today, I'm too tired." And Tatiana would respond sympathetically: "It's crazy that we've been on the ice for so long, you're absolutely right. You must be dead on your feet. But before we go in, why don't you try it this way one time so I can see it?" She kept him interested in what she was doing.

That was the autumn, also, that Sergei finally got the title to his apartment. It was on the fifteenth floor of a building, and I remember the first time he took me up to see it. The people who had just moved out had destroyed it, so it was a very dirty, very dark, very scary studio. It did have a nice balcony, but everything else was ugly and would have to be fixed. It was on this first visit to his apartment that Sergei proposed to me.

It wasn't the way Americans propose to a woman. He didn't invite me to dinner. He didn't give me a ring. He didn't get on his knees and ask me to marry him. Sergei just said, "I would love for you to live with me in this apartment."

He was quite sincere, and to me it was very romantic. Of course we would have to renovate everything in this place before it would be fit to live in. But I could picture how it might one day look, and that Sergei would want me to live with him made me unspeakably happy.

The Wedding

For us, there was a huge difference between competing as amateurs and competing as pros. First of all, in the professional ranks, there's no organizational support. We were used to having teammates, roommates, and a team leader who told us, Here's when and where you eat breakfast, lunch, and dinner. Here's your practice schedule. Here's the bus schedule. Here's your bedtime. Everything.

All of a sudden, Sergei and I had to figure everything out for ourselves. We were late for practices, we missed buses, the ice we practiced on wasn't freshly made. All of it was new. Peter and Kitty Carruthers, the American pairs skaters who'd won a silver medal in the 1984 Olympics, hadn't decided what program they were going to skate until the night before the competition. Then when they did skate, it looked to me almost as if they were making it up as they went along. Paul Theofanous wanted to get together to tell us how interested IMG was in our career, which made us feel added pressure. We had publicity pictures taken at eight o'clock the night before the competition, when I'd normally have been either resting or already in bed.

For me, it was all much more stressful than when we'd skated as amateurs. Meanwhile, everyone else was so friendly and relaxed, always smiling. On the night of the competition, I fell on one of the throws, and in general we didn't skate very well. The Canadian pairs team of Paul Martini and Barbara Underhill beat us. They were fabulous. Then in our second professional competition, in Barcelona, we finished second to Martini and Underhill again. But this time, at least, we skated better. And we won twenty thousand dollars each time out. I was a little upset at being second, but Tatiana told me, "Don't worry. Barbara and Paul know how to present themselves so well, and you will learn." Technical elements are not nearly as important in professional competitions as presentation.

New Year's 1991, we celebrated in Garmisch-Partenkirchen, where they staged an annual ice show. We'd now been in love for two years. The next morning Sergei said to me, "I want to buy you something, Katoosha."

He almost never bought me presents without asking me to help him pick them out, no matter how many times I told him I liked to be surprised. Just give me something, Seriozha. Anything is fine, I'd tell him. But his eyes would become like a little puppy's, and he'd say, "But I want to give you something you want. Please help me. We'll find something together."

So this time we went to an antique jewelry store in Garmisch, and he asked the lady if she had any rings. They didn't have a very big selection, but the lady showed us one we liked, an emerald, with small diamonds on the setting. Sergei bought me this one. The lady was so pleased that she gave me a cross made of rubies. Maybe they weren't real, but they looked like rubies, and I loved this cross. And I especially loved my emerald ring, which I still cannot ever take off.

In Russia we don't have engagement rings. Just wedding rings, which are simple bands of gold. So this emerald ring didn't really mean anything. It just meant Sergei had given me a gift. But later everyone was asking me if it was an engagement ring. And I told them it was, because the wedding was so close.

My mom was overseeing the renovation of Sergei's apartment, which was going to be ready in April. Then, naturally, he would expect us to move in. When I realized that Sergei wasn't going to do anything about getting a wedding license, I took it upon myself to look up in the Russian yellow pages where we could apply for one. Sergei never planned anything. Things just happened naturally with us, but in this instance I helped them along a little bit. In January we went together to this application office, and the lady asked us if we were in a rush or if it would be okay to wait for three months to get the license. We said three months was fine. She looked at her calendar, because the wedding dates were filling up fast, and we ended up choosing April 20.

You know, we should have been so happy that year, because it was the year we were getting married. But in truth that was the only thing we had to be happy about. We just didn't seem to have luck that year. We'd changed coaches, had lost Marina as our choreographer, and were traveling by ourselves. It was all too much for us. Plus, Sergei's shoulder was getting worse and worse. He couldn't do any lifts at all, and couldn't even sleep on his right side. I thought that his skating career might be over.

Paul Theofanous finally got us an appointment to see Dr. Jeff Abrams in Princeton, New Jersey. They did an MRI—magnetic resonance imaging— which was very scary for Sergei, since we had never seen this machine before. He had to lie in this tiny, vibrating, moaning capsule without moving for twenty minutes, just the top of his head sticking out. When the doctor looked at the image, he recommended that he operate arthroscopically on the shoulder in the next couple of days, to clean out the dead tissue and put a miniature camera in there to see just what was wrong.

The operation was set for February 14, Valentine's Day. We were staying in Paul's apartment in

New York, and every day I went for long walks through the city and runs through Central Park. I fell in love with New York during that stay. In other places, life goes on very slowly. But in New York, everyone is walking, everyone is busy, everyone knows exactly where they're going. The people are so solid, so intensely into themselves. They barely acknowledge each other. Always you see them thinking to themselves, talking to themselves. The huge buildings seem to give birth to this great well of adrenaline and energy and power. Life's routine is so much faster and more exciting. Moscow is getting more like that now, but when I was growing up there, people didn't rush anywhere, and everything was much, much calmer. People knew their jobs would still be there when they arrived; their salary would still be paid. No need to rush to the grocery store because you couldn't get anything there anyway.

I even liked the homeless people in New York. At least I liked the homeless man who lived outside Paul's apartment. Paul always said hi to this man, and every morning he gave him a few cigarettes. So Sergei and I became friendly with him, too. We'd talk and smile. Sergei was very shy with high-level persons, but with common people he was quite at ease and open. This homeless man was friendly, and he never asked us for things. Quite the opposite, sometimes he would tell us things he thought we should know. Weird things, maybe, but interesting, too.

On the day Sergei was scheduled for surgery, Paul drove him to Princeton. Sergei didn't really want me to have to wait around the hospital all day. He didn't like me to see him when he was in pain. So I stayed behind to prepare a nice dinner for when they returned. First I went to buy flowers to give to Sergei for Valentine's Day, and that was a crazy experience. The lines in the New York flower stores were so long I couldn't get in, and some of the florists were completely sold out. I was looking for tulips, which were Sergei's favorite. Finally I found some in about the tenth store that I went to, and I also bought candy, fresh fruit, and the ingredients for our meal. I decorated the apartment so everything looked romantic.

They came back around dinnertime. Sergei's arm was in a sling, but otherwise he looked fine. He told me everything had gone well. I gave him the flowers, and he said to me, "Katuuh, do you want to see a movie? We brought you one."

"Okay. If you like."

"It's scary though."

"That's okay. I like scary."

Paul put the tape in the VCR. It was a movie of the surgery they had performed on Sergei. The camera was inside his body. "You see, this is the bad part," Sergei said, pointing to some dead tissue inside his shoulder. "Now the doctor is cleaning it out. Look."

It was quite disgusting. So much for the

romance of my first Valentine's Day in the United States.

The doctor had told Sergei that he had to come back for another surgery, too. He'd discovered the torn rotator cuff, which was a very bad injury. They made the appointment for mid-April, just a few days before our wedding.

Sergei flew back by himself for the second operation. He was only going to be gone a few days, but he had never traveled to America without me—we had traveled so few places alone—and I was very, very worried.

I was busy preparing for the wedding, which was actually going to take place on two different days. The official state-approved wedding was on April 20, when we were scheduled to pick up our license. Then the church wedding, performed by Father Nikolai, and the banquet with all our friends was going to be eight days later, on April 28. Unfortunately, Marina was not going to be able to be there. I called her to tell her the date, but she said she had already signed a contract to coach in Ottawa and was leaving for Canada April 22. She couldn't change her plans, but told me that if I ever needed help, to contact her. And she asked that we not forget her.

Sergei didn't call me after the operation, because he was flying back the next day. When I went to meet his plane, I brought one red rose. I had never gone to meet him at the airport before, and I never would again. This was the only time. He came through the customs line, and his face was so sad. Paul Theofanous had given him two goose down pillows for a wedding present, and Sergei had those pillows under his good arm. His other arm was in a sling, and he had his one small bag slung over his shoulder. He'd been taking the pain pills the doctor had given him, so he looked like he was drunk.

I couldn't help smiling, he looked so funny. I know that wasn't nice, but I was so happy to have him safely home, I couldn't control my smile.

The next morning we had the appointment to get our marriage certificate, and afterward there would be a small party, just for our families. I didn't wear my wedding dress on this day, but once we had the certificate, it meant that we were legally married. Sergei came to pick me up carrying a huge bouquet of roses, but he had forgotten his passport, which he needed to get the license. So he went back to his home to get it, while I went ahead to explain to the officials he would be late. I was worried that if we missed this appointment, it might be another three months before we could get another one.

The ceremony, once Sergei arrived with his passport, was very quick. Yegor was his best man, and my maid of honor was a girl I'd met at Yegor's, also named Katia. I really didn't know her very well, but I couldn't choose my sister, Maria, to be my maid of honor, and I really didn't have any other close girlfriends in my life. Afterward, we celebrated with a small party in my parents' apartment, and the only sad thing about this day was that my Babushka, who was so important to my childhood, was in the hospital, very sick with cancer, and wasn't there.

That was the first night we spent in Sergei's new apartment. He didn't carry me across the threshold—this isn't a custom in Russia—and even if he'd wanted to, he wouldn't have been able to because of his shoulder. He could barely sign for the marriage certificate. The apartment, which I hadn't seen since my mother had renovated it, was beautiful. She had removed the doors between the living room and kitchen, so that now there was a little arch. She'd decorated it with a little table, two armchairs, and a convertible bed that she'd left folded out for us. She'd also left a bottle of champagne on ice, and fresh flowers. This apartment was the best gift she could have offered us: a new world for Seriozha and me.

I felt different. Not more nervous, but I'd been waiting to marry Sergei for such a long time. We had shared our bed in many places before, but now that we were married I was thinking I had to do something different. Something special. I was expecting something like Paris again, I guess. But it wasn't this way. Except that now we had a home in which I could take care of my Seriozha, stay with him and cook his favorite meals.

The church wedding was eight days later. Many of our friends were coming into Moscow from ice shows all over the world. Marina Klimova and

Sergei Ponomarenko, and Maia Usova and Alexander Zhulin came to the restaurant directly from the airport. The speed skater Igor Zhelezovsky was there—Sergei had been his best man. Leonovich. Tatiana Tarasova. Terry Foley had come in from California, and he videotaped the ceremony for us.

The wedding was at 4:00 P.M. at the small church in which I'd been christened. I wore a silk, off-white dress that I'd bought in Toronto, and I was wearing flowers in my hair. It rained all morning and most of the day, which was considered good luck. It doesn't seem like it now. But I was happy that it rained. After saying our vows, we drank champagne in the church, and Father Nikolai sang to our happiness. Then we drove to the restaurant in a white Mercedes that had been loaned to us by the director of Tatiana's show.

At the wedding banquet, everyone kept toasting us, saying "Gorka! Gorka!" which is a signal for the bride and groom to kiss. As long as the guests are still chanting Gorka! you have to keep kissing. It means "bitter," so you have to kiss sweet. The whole wedding people kept saying "Gorka!" A hundred times at least. The only time I remember seeing Sergei that night was when we kissed.

To tell you the truth, I didn't have the greatest time at my wedding. It wasn't the best day for Sergei, either, though Sergei always liked seeing his old friends. He didn't like being the center of attention, and he didn't like it when all the women were asking him to dance. I think people sensed he was a little annoyed, because they didn't do the tradition we have in Russia of stealing the bride and hiding her during the banquet. Then the husband has to pay to get her back.

That night Sergei and I danced our first real waltz. He said, "I don't know how to," and I told him, "I don't either. Let's just try something."

We had skated to two waltzes when we were competing, including the 1989 program in which I pretended to be a young lady dancing the waltz at her first fancy ball; but this was very, very different. We were not good dancers on the floor, I can definitely say this. I was so happy when the banquet was over and we went back to my mother's for a more informal after-party. All the skaters came back, and the apartment was filled with people. Parking was a big problem. Every time someone wanted to leave, he had to come back into the building, take the elevator back up eleven floors, and ask about eight people to move their cars.

Sergei and I were the last to leave. I drove us back to our apartment. I remember thinking, Look at me, chauffering my husband home from *my* wedding. But it was fun, actually, because I was so used to Sergei driving me. It was one more step of married life.

I also remember thinking how much fun it was to be coming home, just the two of us, to our own apartment. How lucky I was to have someone to come home with, someone who would take care of me. That night, for the first time, I really felt married.

At our wedding banquet.

We didn't go on a honeymoon. I don't know why. I don't remember sitting down and discussing it, but I probably thought it was more important to get back onto the ice as soon as possible. That would be typical of the way my mind worked. The way it still works, if I am honest with myself.

The day after the wedding, something sad happened. My mother and I were cleaning the apartment after the party, and a white pigeon flew in through the open window. My father managed to get it out again, but it is a very bad omen in Russia to have a bird fly in your house. It means someone will die. The whole day, my mother was somber and pensive. And that August my dear Babushka died of cancer. She was sixty-two.

We didn't have luck that week. Not a bit of it. Three days after the wedding, I managed to wreck the beautiful Toyota I had bought in Japan, a car that had the steering wheel on the wrong side. Wrong for Russia, anyway, where cars drive on the right side of the road, as they do in America. I am not the world's best driver, I admit. It took me five tries to pass my driving test. But this was an extraordinarily inept performance, even for me. The accident occurred on May 1, which is a big holiday in Russia. Many of the roads are closed, and there are almost no cars on the streets. In fact there was, I believe, only one other driver on the street that morning, and I found him. He was moving too slowly for me. Actually, he was stopped at a red light, but I didn't see it. Maybe I was blinded by the sun. Or the wedding bliss. I don't know, but I crashed right into this car.

The man in the car came to see who was this crazy person who had hit him, and I burst into tears.

"Why are you crying?" he asked. "Did you hurt yourself?"

I told him I hadn't.

"You're okay? Good." Then he said something

odd. "Let's go to my car. I have a little TV inside, and we can watch cartoons."

He didn't seem very upset that I had wrecked his car. I said, "I'm so sorry. I don't know what to say."

"It's all right. It's my friend's car. You know, I looked up and saw you coming, and I tried to move forward, but you got me anyway."

He was right about that. My car was no longer drivable, so I found a phone and called Sergei. "Serioque? I hit a car."

He was silent a moment. "Where did you find this car? The parade is now. No one is on the street."

"Yes, I found the only car. Can you come get me?"

When Sergei arrived I was sitting in the other man's car, watching cartoons on his TV. The man was very apologetic, but since it was his friend's car, he thought he should probably get it fixed before the man returned next month. None of us had insurance. I don't think there was such a thing as insurance in Russia. So Sergei and I paid to have the car fixed, and my father, who had retired from dancing, repaired my Toyota. Fortunately he sold it before I could drive it again.

Newlyweds

Two weeks after the wedding, Sergei's shoulder felt good enough for him to get back on the ice, and by mid-May we had joined Tom Collins's 1991 tour. The fifteen shows we did with Tommy, whom we had come to regard as a friend, were lovely, almost like the honeymoon we never had time for. Life began to move at a faster, more hectic pace. Immediately after the completion of the Collins tour, we went with Tatiana's Russian All-Stars to South Africa, doing twenty shows in Cape Town and Johannesburg. That's where I did the shopping for a lot of furnishings for our new apartment—plates, chandeliers, lamps, sheets, comforters. We also visited a shantytown—very depressing—and went on a safari, where we played with some baby lions. Sergei loved this. He loved all animals. Holding one of the cubs, his face would light up like a child's.

We earned thirty thousand dollars on this South African tour, and I remember Paul Theofanous told us to give the money to two ladies who worked for IMG, and they would transfer the money back to the United States. That way we wouldn't have to pay duty on it back in Russia. We had never met these ladies before. They came to our hotel in Johannesburg, we gave them the money, and they left without even giving us a receipt. Sergei and I just looked at each other in disbelief. What did we just do? our expressions said. But it turned out all right. The money got home. But Sergei and I were not at all experienced in financial matters. We had no training, and no one was offering it.

That summer Tatiana created a *West Side Story* program for us. For the first time, she was making Sergei act. He always did choreography, the movements with his arms and his hands, but he had never acted before. In *West Side Story*, he had to pretend to die. That was a huge step for Sergei. Me, I liked to act. I'd been acting since I was a little girl at the dacha, creating productions like *Borahtino* for our neighbors. But not Sergei, and he definitely didn't like it. He'd say to me, "Next thing you know, she'll make me kill someone on the ice." But he respected her enough to do it.

Another time she made a terrible program for us from *Opera Piazza*, sung by Placido Domingo, in which we both dressed up as clowns, all white, even the faces. I painted Sergei's face, and made it with a tear rolling down his cheek. It was our artistic program for one season of professional competitions, and I still can't believe Sergei agreed to go along with it. He had no pretenses when he skated. There was nothing false about him, and he never let us drop to a level lower than he thought we could skate. Graceful and understated, he used to say, "I am a skater. I don't want to make a joke on myself."

On the ice, everyone may have been watching me, but it was only because Sergei showed me off. He was so proud of me. Yet he was always the stronger person, the one who never missed an element. His skating had both honesty and subtlety. He showed the audience no more than it needed to know. To dress such a man up like a harlequin, to paint his face like a clown's, was to mask all his best skills as a skater and artist. Somehow, however, he was able to pull this program off. I was worried everyone would laugh at us in these clown suits, but they didn't. And we won with this program, too.

Tatiana had so much life experience and skating experience. She was like a mother to her skaters, a little like Galina Zmievskaya, and Sergei and I were at a time in our lives when we felt we needed someone who would care about us and our health. When we were amateurs, it was always you need to do this, you need to do that. No one ever asked us what we wanted. But Tatiana did. She had started to coach when she was just eighteen or nineteen, and she was always teaching us new steps, giving us new things to try. When she created a program, she had it all visualized before even stepping out on the ice. I don't know if this was good or not, because if you can visualize it in your mind, you've probably already seen it. It may not be entirely original. Marina never worked this way.

Around this time, we had heard that Toller Cranston, the Canadian skater, coach, and choreographer, wanted to create a program for us. We still needed a free-skating program for the 1991 Professional Championships in Landover, so we flew to Toronto in the fall to work with him. He already had music from *The Nutcracker* picked out, and we liked it immediately. I have always liked to skate to Tchaikovsky. Then it was, do this, do this, maybe do this. We were so surprised at the way he worked. He also sketched the costumes for us. But after only two days, he had to leave to go to an exhibition. We couldn't believe it. We'd paid all this money to fly there, more money for ice time and the hotel. Then two sessions and goodbye. We were pretty upset.

But Ellen Burka, who was Toller's assistant, said, "Don't worry. I'll finish the program for him." And we ended up winning the World Professional Championships with this *Nutcracker* program, in 1991 and again in 1992.

Christopher Bowman was also training with Toller at that time, and one day he came to practice with a big bruise on his eye. It made all the papers how he'd been beaten up under mysterious circumstances, and there was a lot of speculation about drugs. But that day Ellen made him skate with his swollen eye, all black and blue, and was telling him he had to "smile like a million-dollar bill." Ellen was putting on his music, and I was thinking, Why are you bothering? He's totally out of it. He doesn't even know his program.

Sergei and I always heard rumors about drug use, especially during the tours, but I can truthfully say I never saw anyone use drugs in front of me. I didn't care what was going on with Christopher Bowman, but because Sergei was friendly with him, one time I asked Sergei if he had ever tried drugs or not. He said no, that he had no interest in them.

Training in Toronto that fall was fun. Difficult, but fun. We had to figure everything out by ourselves—how to take the subway, where to do our shopping. No one was there to translate for us. My English had gotten much better, but it was still not very good, and because Sergei didn't speak English at all it was quite stressful for me. But we liked this feeling of independence, of looking after each other.

Nineteen ninety-one was a year of big changes for us. We hadn't really known what stress was before. Pressure, yes. But stress is different from pressure. Now suddenly I was in charge of airplane tickets, the passports, the cash. I was afraid we might board a plane and fly to the wrong city. I worried what would happen if the airline lost our bags.

I especially worried every time we flew to the Frankfurt airport, which was where many flights connected both into and out of Moscow. I hated this airport. One time I lost my silver fox fur coat there when it fell off my pushcart. I don't know how I could have walked right over it, but I did. Some nice people picked it up off the floor and brought it to the nearest cafeteria, and when Sergei and I retraced our steps, the cafeteria manager was holding my coat for me. Very lucky. Another time I left my wallet at a shop in the Frankfurt airport, and they had to page me to return for it. Also lucky. Once I even lost Sergei, for heaven's sake.

We were supposed to meet at a certain place at a certain time, since we had a plane to catch for Moscow. I went to this place, the time passed, and there was still no Sergei. I started looking for him. I searched and searched the airport. The thoughts that came into my head began to get very weird.

Why does Sergei want to stay in Frankfurt? I wondered. Why doesn't he want to go with me? He had taken his passport with him shopping, which was unusual, and also his airplane ticket. Usually I held onto those. The more I thought about it, the worse it began to seem. Why does Seriozha want to leave me? I asked myself. I finally found him at the gate just before the plane took off for Moscow. They had been paging me. Sergei told me to never, ever go looking for him. "If I tell you a place for us to meet," he said, "just stay there until I find you." I was so relieved that he wasn't leaving me after all that I didn't mind that he was angry. He could have said anything.

That was the first year we skated with Stars on Ice. We began rehearsing in the fall in Aspen, and it was an exciting change to be working with all the other skaters: Brian Orser, Scott Hamilton, Debi Thomas, Rosalynn Sumners, Peter and Kitty Carruthers. We skated in several group numbers, and I had to translate for Sergei during the rehearsals. Everyone was friendly and very relaxed. If you wanted to, you could go wild on the ice during rehearsals, which was quite a new thing for us.

The thing we liked most about Aspen was a bookstore we found that was also a library and a place where you could get something to eat or drink. We had never seen a place like this. Sergei loved all bookstores. Since he didn't read English, he would spend entire afternoons looking through the beautiful coffee table picture books. But in this place, Sergei could go upstairs, where there was a fireplace, and spend an entire evening looking at books and magazines. They had couches and armchairs to sit in, very comfortable and cozy, and every night we would order a glass of port, maybe a dessert, and just relax.

Sergei and I were learning a new program created by Sarah Kawahara, and there was one tricky part where I had to do a back flip with Sergei's help. While we were practicing it, my skate blade hit Sergei in the head, and he began bleeding quite badly. I got so scared I started to cry.

"Why are *you* crying?" Sergei asked me.

We took him to the hospital, and before they would fix him, they began asking us questions. Of course Sergei didn't understand any of these questions, so I was translating for him, and it was taking a long time. I kept interjecting: "Why can't you help him? He's bleeding all over your hospital." But no, the questions must come first. I didn't understand medicine in this country at the time.

The saddest thing about that fall was that Rob McCall was very sick with AIDS. He was the Canadian ice dancer who had won a bronze medal with Tracy Wilson at the Calgary Olympics. Brian Orser had to leave rehearsals a couple of times to go visit him in the hospital. I remember that Brian and Rob used to sit in the back of the bus when we were on tour after the Olympics, which is also where Sergei and I liked to sit. We sat there out of habit from the days when Zhuk coached us, because Zhuk always sat in the front of the bus, and we wanted to be as far away from him as possible. Brian and Rob sat there because they were always the last two on the bus. They were always laughing, and I remember Rob used to get so excited whenever he bought new clothes. He had a fun personality. I used to like to watch him skate in practices because he was always creating new steps for himself and Tracy, just for the joy of it. He loved skating, and never felt as great as he did when he was on the ice. Rob died before the show opened, and when the tour got to Toronto, we did a benefit in his memory for a hospital specializing in AIDS research.

Going on this tour was so different from our amateur days. We opened that year in Great Falls, Montana, I think, and the finale wasn't ready until the actual day of the show. Everything was always coming together at the last second. It was hard to keep all the cities and towns straight, places like Muskegon, Fort Wayne, East Lansing, Kalamazoo, Erie, and Binghamton. Not exactly Paris or Copenhagen.

But we never really got tired of life on the road. The hotels were always nice, sometimes even beautiful, and in each city we discovered our favorite restaurants. We saw friends all over the country who had moved from Russia, and Sergei loved to go to hockey games whenever we could, which was pretty often. I hated the suitcases, wearing the same outfits for months at a time, packing them up after a late show and a reception, sometimes leaving at two o'clock in the morning. Those receptions were never fun: sitting at a table and signing autographs for the sponsors and their friends as they walked in. They're all eating food, drinking, and you have to sign while you're sitting there hungry and thirsty.

The Stars on Ice bus was fun, though. It had

On the road during our first Stars on Ice tour.

bunk beds, a small kitchen, two televisions, a refrigerator, and several couches. It was a good spot to talk and relax. But I must say, I missed cooking whenever we were on tour. I even missed cleaning. Sometimes at restaurants I felt like going into the kitchen and saying, "Excuse me. Can I help you with something? Washing the dishes, maybe?"

We finished that tour in the late fall of 1991, won our first World Professional Championships in December, then flew back to Moscow to rejoin the

Russian All-Stars. Tatiana had booked us for some performances in Spain, but when we got down there, something went wrong, and the show was canceled. We ended up staying in a little hotel outside Barcelona, waiting for this mix-up to be straightened out. We stayed there two weeks, playing soccer, drinking wine, eating delicious food. But we were not getting paid. Not four thousand dollars a week. Not a dime. Tatiana kept telling us that any day now it all would be settled.

Finally Sergei told Tatiana we couldn't wait any longer. We had the New Year's show coming up in Garmisch-Partenkirchen again, and for that we were definitely being paid five thousand dollars. Paul Theofanous, meanwhile, kept sending us faxes at this little hotel, telling us to leave because he had work for us elsewhere. But the faxes never arrived, because there was only one person who worked at the hotel, and he didn't know how to work the machine. We ended up having to take a train out of there to Madrid, then having to buy expensive business-class tickets to Moscow in order to get there in time to get a visa for Germany. So many problems I don't even remember. And that, unfortunately, marked the end of our working relationship with Tatiana Tarasova.

A Gift

We always had a problem deciding where to go after the end of one tour and before the start of another. It was a lot of trouble flying back and forth to Moscow, and we didn't have a home in the United States. After Garmisch, the Stars on Ice tour picked up again in mid-January, and in the interim Sergei and I decided to spend ten days with Lynn and Bill Plage near Denver. Lynn handled the publicity for the tour, and the Plages were old friends of Scott Hamilton.

To get around, we borrowed a huge old car from some friends of the Plages, a Lincoln Continental, which was bigger than anything either Sergei or I had been in. It was quite a confusing automobile. You had to turn the radio off when you parked it, or the battery would go dead, which happened to us on two different occasions.

One night we drove to Denver to see Brian Boitano and Katarina Witt's show, and on the way back to the Plages' we got lost. You know how when you are lost and looking for turns, maybe you don't pay so much attention to the speed you are going? Well, this must have happened, because suddenly a police car was behind us with its light flashing. But no siren. We didn't know anything about this rule, so we kept driving. In Moscow the police cars always turn on the siren. Finally this Denver police car played its siren. Then Sergei stopped.

It was a woman police officer, and she came around to Sergei's side of the car. He handed her his Russian driving license. She started asking him questions, but the car was so huge I couldn't hear what they were, so I couldn't translate. I tried to tell her he didn't speak English, but she couldn't hear me either. I had to start yelling.

She said, "What? What are you saying?"

I got out of the car so we could stop yelling at each other. Then things got very scary. She reached for her gun and screamed at me, "Get back in the car!" Something so rude. I wasn't used to people speaking to me this way. I didn't know this rule about not getting out of the car, and now she was threatening to shoot me.

Finally she calmed down and came around to my side, and I explained we were figure skaters who were lost. She recognized us then but told us we couldn't drive this huge car anymore. She said to get in her police car, and she would drive us home. But first she wanted to take us back to the station to introduce us to her friends. Of course we agreed to do this. It didn't seem as if we had a choice.

❖   ❖   ❖

At the end of January, I started to feel strange. We were touring with Stars, and we used to have our dinners in the afternoon between the practice and the evening show. All of a sudden, I couldn't even smell the food. I was hungry for it, too. The next day, I couldn't smell coffee, and I love the smell of coffee.

I wondered what was going wrong with me, and immediately thought, Maybe I'm pregnant. I wasn't trying to get pregnant, but I wasn't using birth control, either. If that sounds crazy, I don't really have an explanation. As I've said, Sergei and I never really planned anything.

When Sergei and I returned to Moscow during a break in the Stars on Ice tour, I talked to my mom right away. I hadn't said anything to Sergei. I was too shy to tell him what I suspected. My mother took me to the hospital, and they gave me a series of tests, and sure enough, I was pregnant.

My first thought was, I don't want to have the baby. I was so young—twenty—and I was worried about missing a whole year of skating. So I told my mother, "Let's make an appointment, because I probably should have an abortion."

She listened and said she'd talk to the doctors about this appointment. She wanted me to wait for her in the hallway, and she went to see them by herself.

It wasn't until much later that she told me what she did. She knew I wasn't going to listen only to her, and that I could be very stubborn when I set my mind on something. So she went to the head doctor and convinced him to tell me that an abortion would be dangerous.

This doctor came back a little later to where I was waiting and explained to me very gently that if I had an abortion now, there was a good chance I'd never be able to have any more children. He cited the example of a famous Russian ballerina to whom this had happened, and this example made me afraid. He said it was too early to schedule such an operation anyway, since I was only three weeks pregnant. Even if I still wanted the abortion, we'd have to wait another three weeks. So we left it that I'd go home to think about it.

My mother came back and asked me what the doctor had said. I told her they were concerned it might be a problem, and she said, "Yes, that's a good point. It might be a problem. Maybe you should also talk to Father Nikolai about this question."

I was very confused and undecided. I was scared of this operation, and also a little bit excited at the idea of being pregnant. That night I still said nothing about the pregnancy to Sergei. He was out late with some of his friends, which upset me, of course, and the next morning I was still angry with him. I felt sick, and somehow we got into a silly argument. I don't remember what it was about, but my hormones must have been making me crazy, because I suddenly blurted out, "I'm pregnant. I'm feeling bad, and you don't even care. You could have had a baby, but I'm going to go have an abortion now."

Sergei was shocked. "Is it true? What are you talking about?" He forgot that I was mad at him, forgot the argument, forgot even the talk of an abortion. "Why didn't you tell me before?" He was so excited, and kept holding me and kissing me. "Why didn't you tell me, Katoosh?"

We called my mother, and the three of us went to another hospital. I think my mother wanted another opinion, to make sure I wasn't too little to have a baby. They did the tests all over again, and I learned my due date was September 20.

I remember coming back from these tests and seeing my mother and Sergei sitting in the hall with these big grins on their faces. They were so happy. Meanwhile, I was worrying: We're going to miss a whole year. We're not going to skate. What's going to happen to my body? How am I going to get back in shape?

The first child is scary for a woman. But all they were thinking about was the baby. "We're going to have a baby," Seriozha kept saying, touching me and holding my hand. He looked like a cat lying on its back in the sun. And my mother, too, was excited, saying: "I'm going to have a grandchild." So there were no more decisions to be made. I was happy that they were happy, and they were so sure about my having the baby. Even my father thought it was a good idea. My mom had been twenty when she had me, and he said it's better to have children when you're young and have energy.

I went to talk to Father Nikolai, who has five children of his own. He told me, "It's so important that you have this first child, because it's a gift to you from God." He asked if we had been using birth control, which is not sanctioned by the Russian Orthodox church. I told him we had not. Father Nikolai said, "After you have this child, then you can use birth control. But this first one is a real child from God, because it is a child born from love."

Sergei and I didn't tell anyone else. I remember staying at home and watching the Olympic Games in Albertville on television, and being so nervous and excited for our friends Marina Klimova and Sergei Ponomarenko, who after a bronze and a silver, finally won a gold medal in ice dancing. Tatiana had helped get them ready, and it was truly a gorgeous program, intricate and flowing and dramatic. Afterward we called them to congratulate them. Watching them skate was what really made me want to compete in the Olympics again. It was the first time this thought settled in my head.

In the pairs, Natalia Mishkutenok and Artur

Dmitriev, the Russian pair from Saint Petersburg, were good. I liked their short program very much, and was happy for them that they won. A part of me wished I was there, although I knew, because we had turned professional, it was impossible. I wasn't very sad, not terribly. I never said to Sergei that I thought it was too bad we weren't competing. But after watching the other pairs skaters I did think that we still had the energy and technical skills to compete with anyone. And Sergei was thinking the same thing. We had heard that Brian Boitano had written a letter to the International Skating Union, requesting that professionals be allowed to compete in the next Olympics, which were just two years away. So we knew there was at least a glimmer of hope we'd be able to come back. But Sergei and I didn't discuss it.

I remember quite well that the first person, outside the family, to congratulate us on my pregnancy was Paul Theofanous. Sergei told him, and Paul's immediate reaction was, "Great! Congratulations! You're going to be a father!"

This is very American. In Moscow, the attitude is quite different. The reaction of friends is more like, "Oh, you're pregnant. Lots of work ahead." It's not bad news, but it's certainly not something that you congratulate someone about the way people do in America. It says a great deal about what kind of life people in Russia expect.

We told Paul that I wanted to keep skating in the Stars on Ice show as long as possible. When we returned to the States after the Olympic break, Byron Allen, the producer of the show, took me to a hospital for another set of tests, and here they told us that we were having a baby girl. I thought it was a boy. I was sure of it, in fact. I believed the doctors weren't seeing it well.

I'd only had morning sickness one time, but my body was definitely changing. I couldn't drink coffee or eat chocolate, and I couldn't figure out why I was always so weak, why I got tired so fast. I used to get mad at myself when I couldn't skate through a whole program without getting exhausted. We were still doing our *Nutcracker* long program in the show, plus another number, plus three group numbers, and I was so tired by the end. Every night I flopped into my bed thinking, Oh, this feels great. I'm going to have so much energy tomorrow. But I never did.

I couldn't get it into my head all that was entailed in having a baby. I didn't expect my body to grow so fast, and I got so upset when I couldn't fit into my skating costume. I was crying in my dressing room. Lynn Plage was trying to help me with my emotions. I fell a couple of times doing the triple salchow throw, so we changed it to a double salchow throw. Also, I was thinking I shouldn't eat a lot or I'd gain too much weight. It was just stupid, but it was a lot for me to handle then. I was worried about whether or not I could finish the tour.

Sergei, though, was definitely very happy. He

held me all the time, and hugged me, and tried to feel the baby in my belly. He was talking about the baby all the time. We decided to name her Daria, since my mother had told me years before that if she had had a third girl, she'd have named it Daria. Ekaterina, Maria, then Daria. And Sergei liked this name very much.

When the tour got to Toronto, Barbara Underhill came to see us. She had taken the season off, because she was pregnant, too, only she was expecting twins. I thought at the time that nobody knew that Sergei and I were expecting a baby, but of course everyone did. Barbara, when she saw me, ran up and lifted her shirt to show me her big belly, and said, "Oh, Katia, show me yours!" I was so shocked. Barbara was telling me, "Oh, you're so thin. Katia, you're still skating. Are you okay?" She made me feel a little bit brave.

When we got to Ottawa, I called Marina and asked if she'd like to see the show. Then I told her I was four months pregnant. "Oh, it's good," she said right away. "You're going to be a mommy. And afterward you will skate again."

That made me feel better. We arranged to meet with her before the show, and we saw where she was living and the rink where she coached. It was the first time we'd seen Marina since she'd left Russia a year earlier.

I made it through until the end of the Canadian tour, and in the last Stars on Ice practice, in Halifax, I did some double axels, just for my own satisfaction. Once I got back to Moscow, I knew, there'd be no more skating until after the baby was born.

All the other skaters gave me a baby shower. I still didn't think they all knew I was pregnant, and when I walked in, I blushed and thought, *Everyone* knows. We don't have this tradition of baby showers in Russia. They gave me three mugs, Mama Bear's, Papa Bear's, and Baby Bear's; a mirror with a yardstick on it to measure the baby; and Rosalynn Sumners gave Daria a music box with dancing bears inside. So many fun presents. I was so touched by these gifts. It was a real celebration of life.

Daria

Sergei and I spent a wonderful summer in Moscow getting ready to have the baby. By now I was proud of myself for being pregnant, and was carefully monitoring what I was eating. I was walking and exercising every day. Sometimes I would walk up all fifteen flights of stairs to our apartment, which was extremely boring. I listened to music, which was good for my state of mind. I had never pampered myself in this manner before.

Everyone was so surprised I was having a baby, and they pampered me, too. Sit here, Katia. Are you comfortable? Will you have something to eat? Sergei, too, was taking care of me so tenderly, watching to make sure I was eating enough. He was always very careful not to make me mad, and was considerate of all my needs.

It was a very hot summer in Moscow, too hot

sometimes to walk in the middle of the day. I never liked the hot weather, so I'd wait until it cooled down, sometimes after midnight. Then I'd ask Sergei, Can you come with me? He said for me to go ahead, and he promised to watch me walk from the balcony. Which he did. I could see him. I don't know what good he thought he'd be able to do, since we lived on the fifteenth floor. He did own a bow and arrow. Maybe that would have helped.

One meal he said to me, "Katuuh, did you have a good lunch?" I told him I had. He said, "Finish this black caviar sandwich, and I'll give you a surprise." Everyone told me I should eat caviar because of the protein. So I finished the sandwich, and I was so full. Then Sergei brought me a big box. There was a nice scarf inside, and inside the scarf was a beautiful Rolex watch. I was totally shocked. I lost my voice I was so surprised, because Sergei never gave me surprise presents.

I told him, "Thank you, Seriozha. I don't deserve this. I'll probably lose it."

And he told me something so sweet: "No, you deserve more than this. This is just a gift."

Although the gift made me very happy, the way Seriozha treated me, so gently, so lovingly, made me even happier.

In June or July, Sergei got a new pair of skating boots, and he went on the ice to break them in. Just for fun, I went too. I kept tipping forward and backward on the ice, since my center of balance had completely changed. It was as if I had completely lost my coordination. But I didn't even worry about it for once. I was only worried about my health and my baby.

Sergei took me on a fifteen-day trip through Davos, Zurich, and Greece, just the two of us, and it was the most lovely vacation. Greece was so beautiful, and I remember Sergei watching me one time when the baby was kicking. "What's going on inside your stomach?" he asked.

"You want to feel?" I took his hand and laid it on my belly, and he felt it, too. Daria kicking hello to her dad.

I gained eighteen pounds during the pregnancy, which was all right. But Tatiana recommended I go to this certain hospital that specialized in problem births, just to be on the safe side. So I did, and they examined me and told me that because of my small size, they'd probably have to give me a cesarean.

I talked to my mom about this, and she said that a cesarean would probably be okay. But of course the healing process would be quite long. I wasn't happy with this cesarean idea, and for the first time, I started wondering if we should have our baby in the United States. We called Paul Theofanous, and he wanted to know what we were going to do next season, whether IMG could count on us for Stars on Ice or not. Rehearsals were going to start at the end of October, five weeks after the baby was due. If I had a cesarean, it

Daria, born in New Jersey,
September 11, 1992.

would be impossible to make these rehearsals, and
we might miss the entire season. Like a true Gemini, I vacillated about what to do. One day I

thought I should fly to the United States to have the baby, the next day I would decide it was all right to have it in Moscow.

Sergei and I finally decided we should have the baby in America. Paul found a doctor for us near his home in Morristown, New Jersey, and rented a condominium where we could stay, and Sergei and I bought airplane tickets for August 26. But when we went to the airport, we found out that our visas had expired. We couldn't leave.

I was so upset, as you can imagine. Sergei exchanged the tickets for another day, but now we had to go to the American embassy to get visas for us and for my mother, who was going to come later in the month to help us when the baby was born.

I tried to dress so that the baby didn't show, and it's true that most people couldn't tell that I was pregnant. We walked into this guy's office, and he greets us with, "Hello, hello, come right in. Now tell me, why do you want to have your baby in the United States?"

His first question! I started to explain about rehearsals, how we had to get right onto the ice and practice for the show. He said, "And what about your baby having U.S. citizenship? What do you think about that?"

I told him that would be okay, but that it wasn't our main reason. He asked us to wait. While he went to talk to someone, I was so scared he would tell us we couldn't go. But when he came back, he gave us the visas.

Then it was the doctors at the hospital who told us we were too late, that if we were going to leave, we should have flown earlier in August. So of course I was a little nervous when we left September 1. But I was convinced I'd be fine, and that Daria would behave by staying where she was until my due date on the twentieth.

The day after landing in the States, we went to see the obstetrician that Paul had found for us, and, again, I was told the baby was going to be a girl. The doctor also said that the baby was not going to grow anymore, and that the next week we could have the delivery induced. We made an appointment to do this on the thirteenth of September.

Paul asked if we'd like to see the U.S. Open tennis tournament, and we told him yes, of course. He got us great seats for the evening matches the night of September 10, and it was fantastic, like being at the theater. Unfortunately, they had to stop the match when it started to rain in buckets, and we could barely get to the car, jumping through puddles on the way.

That night I felt a little more achy than usual, and Sergei drove home without any help from me, since I wasn't paying attention. In the middle of the night, about 4:00 A.M., I woke up feeling very weird. After an hour of walking around the condominium, I started having contractions. But I didn't know what they were. No one had prepared me for this. I felt bad, then okay; bad, then okay. I thought this was very odd, and in the moments when I was feeling okay I began to carefully read the pamphlet that the doctor had given me on our last visit. That's when I realized I was probably having contractions.

I called the hospital, and they said I should come over. Then I woke Sergei, who began rushing around. The contractions were coming stronger and stronger, shorter and shorter apart. It made him very nervous to hear me in the car: "I'm okay, I'm okay," then, "Aaarrrggghhh." Poor guy, he didn't know what to do. I told him to just get me to the emergency entrance, which he did, because we'd practiced this drive many times with Paul.

The receptionist checked me in, and once I appeared to be in good hands, Sergei said, "I'll just go wait in the car." He didn't want to have to sit in the waiting room and be asked a lot of questions that he couldn't answer. This was the worst for him. And there was no question of him helping with the delivery, which in Russia a man didn't do.

They put me in a room, which was a little scary because the woman next door was already scream-ing. My doctors gave me a shot in the shoulder, and I briefly fell asleep. Then the contractions came back again, and the pain was becoming stronger and stronger. I was asked if I wanted a shot in the spine to kill the pain.

We hadn't talked about any of this before, so the doctor explained the options to me. Finally I said yes, give me the shot. Right now. But then they gave me a lot of papers that I was told I must read and sign first. I am thinking, What? Are they crazy? They want me to sign a contract? Give me this shot. But no, I must read this and sign. It is, of course, in English, and I am not thinking now in English. The only thing I understand is if I sign this contract, the pain goes away. Maybe the car, too. Maybe the Rolex. I don't care. Give me this shot.

Which they did. Into the back, which I wasn't expecting, although I'm sure it was all carefully explained in the document. And then everything is nice and I'm totally relaxed.

Finally, around 11:00 A.M., they asked some questions about Sergei. "Isn't your husband going to be here with you?"

"What for?" I asked. "Is this necessary? Can't he wait in the car?"

"What about a girlfriend?" the nurse asked.

"What girlfriend?" I said. "No one told me I needed to bring a girlfriend to have my baby."

Then the nurse said, "We're telling you, you need to have someone here with you. We're going to get your husband. He's the only one who can speak to you in Russian. What kind of car is he in?"

I told them, and the nurse found the car. Sergei was asleep inside. She tapped on the window, motioning for him to follow her. He totally misunderstood. Oh, already done? Great. Is it a boy or girl? He was rushing behind the nurse and was very surprised when he came into the room to see the baby was not born yet.

But Sergei looked calm, as he always did. Not nervous. I was the one who was nervous. I said to him, "They said you had to be with me, Serioque. Is that okay?"

"Yes, of course. Are you in very great pain, Katoosha?"

I couldn't feel a thing, but I didn't think I should tell him that. "No," I said. "As a matter of fact, I feel fine."

He was actually happy to stay. He kept kissing my hand. The doctor started to show Sergei the machines that were monitoring my progress, and the baby's, all the waves that measured the strength of the contractions. Sergei listened to him politely. Then the doctor was telling me to push and push.

I was shaking all over, really shivering, I think from a reaction to the shot in the spine. I didn't remember to push. Sergei was holding my hand. Three or four times I pushed, and the only thing I felt was when Daria came out. It was like everything in my body below my neck came out, too. I now felt completely empty.

The doctor put Daria on my stomach, and I was still shaking like crazy, very, very cold. And I remember thinking, Wow, is everybody going to be surprised when they see that it's a boy. I still didn't believe them. But I was the one who was surprised.

"She's a girl," the doctor said, and he gave Daria to Sergei to hold, before I even had a chance to hold her. Sergei was so shocked, but he took her. He didn't even have a hospital gown on, like everyone else. He was standing there in his blue-jean shirt. I can still picture them. And I was so happy now that he was there. Daria was so small, and red, and she didn't have any hair. They cleaned her up and put this funny little hat on her head, and they asked if we wanted to call home.

To Moscow?

They said sure. Of course. So we called home, and when my mother picked up the phone, Sergei said, "Hello, Grandma."

"Already?" she cried. She wasn't coming for another week and thought she'd be there in time to explain all these things about having a baby to me.

Daria weighed five pounds, four ounces, and was in perfect health. But she was by far the smallest baby in the observation room. And every other baby in there had a full head of hair. The fact that she had no hair drove me crazy. I don't know why. That first night I was so upset that I cried all night long. I was thinking, I did a bad job. I didn't eat properly, I skated too long, and that's why Daria has no hair. I was such a sad, funny little mom, and very far from home.

Leaving

*S*ergei went back to the condominium from the hospital and drank an entire bottle of champagne. Then he called everyone that we knew. All night long he made phone calls, telling people that Daria was going to be a tennis player, because she was so interested in watching the U.S. Open that she came early.

He brought flowers and gifts when he visited me the next day, and when, three days later, I went home from the hospital, he was all the time hugging me and kissing me, all the time taking pictures of me and Daria. I had never seen him so happy. And every time I suggested someone we should call—Yegor or Fadeev, maybe—he'd answer, "Oh, Katuuh, we don't have to, because I've already called them." He'd rung up a very big bill.

We were both looking forward to my mom coming to stay with us, because I was still unsure at times what I was doing. There were no problems, fortunately. The breast-feeding was going fine, and Sergei and I had watched the nurse change the diapers, so we were able to try this delicate procedure together. When I left him alone a couple of times with Daria as she slept, he asked me nervously what to do if she woke up. I told him I didn't know. And I didn't.

It was a big load off my mind when my mom finally arrived. I was still worried about Daria being so small and having such red skin and no hair. I started complaining to her about Daria's appearance, and she told me to be quiet, that I was a scarier looking baby than Daria. She said that Daria was just beautiful.

Mom showed us how to do everything: burp Daria, give her baths, change her clothes. When Daria was crying sometimes, Mom would peel a grape and put it in cheesecloth, and she would let Daria suck it. This always quieted her down. Every day there was some small change. One day she'd move her eyes. The next day she'd move her legs. The first bath. The first smile. All the time we were thanking God that He had brought us such happiness.

Twelve days after Daria was born, on September 23, Sergei took me to the gym to work out for the first time, and we started going back every day. So when Jay Ogden came to the condomini-

A family of three.

um to find out if we were going to be ready to skate that season, we told him we would. Rehearsals were starting in a month.

Sergei wanted me to ask Jay for more money. "Ask him, Katuuh," he prodded. I tried, but you know, I can't ask these questions about money. The words actually wouldn't come out of my mouth. If Sergei had been the one to speak English, he would have done all our negotiating. But he didn't, so it was left up to me. I finally managed to say something like, "Do you think it might be a possibility to consider letting us earn a little more money now that we have a baby?" Jay listened to this question, then reminded me that IMG had a choice of which pairs skaters to invite for their tour, and hoped that we would accept their offer. That was the note we left on. We didn't decide anything then.

In the end we agreed to return for the same money we'd been making before. On the thirtieth of September I finally skated again, nineteen days after Daria was born and about six months since landing those double axels in my last practice in Halifax. I was falling down every time I tried to jump, and I was also having some back pain. But it was a thrill to be on the ice again.

Our new, small family was so happy. It was beautiful in New Jersey in the fall, and we took Daria for walks in the nearby park. When she was one month old, we had her picture taken for her American passport. The poor little thing could not even hold her head up for this photograph, and you can see, in the passport photo, Sergei's fingers propping her head up from behind. In his big hands, she looks like a tiny bird. Daria will remain a dual citizen of Russia and the United States until she is eighteen, and then she has to decide.

Rehearsals for Stars on Ice were in Lake Placid that year. They began the nineteenth of October, and before we left New Jersey, we had to decide what to do with Daria. We didn't want to keep her in a hotel, where IMG had gotten rooms for the skaters, and no one suggested to us that we take a condominium or rent a house in Lake Placid. In future years, we insisted on this, but at the time we didn't think of it. No one said to us, "Would you like to bring Daria, too? We can find a place with a kitchen." We should have asked, I know. But we didn't. We were just happy Stars on Ice took us back, and it was very important that we didn't lose another year of skating. So we decided we couldn't take Daria with us because we had to work.

This is why most skaters don't have babies. Very few do while they're still performing. You have a year off the ice, and it's difficult to bring your body back. Then you're traveling all the time without your baby. If Daria had been born in early summer, we'd have had more time to be with her after she was born. Or if Sergei had been a singles skater and had been able to make money by himself, maybe I'd have been able to stop skating and concentrate on being a mom. But he couldn't skate without me. And my dad was retired, living on a pension. And my mom had very limited possibilities to earn money.

So my mom quit her job and told me, "I'm at your disposal; I still have enough energy; I will take care of Daria. Now you can go back to work. You're young, and you love your work. Better that you should miss Daria than that she has to follow you around the country living in hotels."

That was the thinking, but it was driving me crazy that I wasn't going to be a mom to my baby daughter. What choice, though, was there? We could quit skating to be with Daria, have no money, live like all Russian people back in Moscow, and someday coach. Or we could skate and let my mom raise Daria. That was the choice.

My mother decided that she would take Daria to visit Terry Foley's family in California while we were in Lake Placid. That way she wouldn't be alone in New Jersey. We weaned Daria from my breast milk and put her on the bottle, and on the seventeenth we drove my mom and Daria to the airport. She was just five weeks old.

It was okay until they had gone. But afterward, when Sergei and I sat in the car, I never had such a terrible feeling before. It was like half of my heart had gone away. It was the same with Sergei. We didn't talk. We didn't say anything to each other. Then we realized we were driving exactly the wrong direction home from the airport. We were seeing signs for Atlantic City. It didn't matter, we both felt so empty and sad. When I made the decision to let my mom take my baby, I didn't think it would be so terrible. And when we got home I just lay down on my bed and cried.

My mom called that night. She made me feel better by telling me they had arrived safely and that everything was fine. There were lots of toys at Terry's house for Daria. So I was in slightly better spirits when Sergei and I drove to Lake Placid to start rehearsals.

Every day we were on the ice from 10:00 A.M. to 6:00 P.M. I was still very weak, but we were both hungry for skating. Sergei's shoulder felt good, and the lifts were going okay. Michael Seibert, who'd been an ice dancer with his partner, Judy Blumberg, was creating two new programs for us, and it was the first time we'd worked with Michael. He could lift me without a problem, and would show all these dance lifts to Sergei. He also gave us lots of new steps to learn. It was fun for us, and I began getting stronger. We even started doing our triple twist again.

Jay Ogden came to Lake Placid that fall, and we agreed to be paid the same money as the year before. Then he told us that for the World Professional Championships in Landover in December, he could get us an appearance guarantee of twenty thousand dollars from the organizers. The prize money at these championships was forty thousand dollars for first, thirty thousand for second, and

Irene Ersek

Back on the ice after Daria's birth.

twenty thousand for third. Four pairs had been invited, all Russians: Elena Bechke and Denis Petrov; Natalia Mishkutenok and Artur Dmitriev; Elena Valova and Oleg Vassiliev; and us. Sergei told Jay, "We don't need this guarantee. It's impossible for us to finish lower than third." You should have seen the look on Jay's face. He thought he was doing such a great job for us. But that's how confident Sergei was that we were once again healthy.

I was still heavyhearted from having left Daria. I was worried that she wouldn't remember me as her mother, that she'd forget me entirely, even. All her life, I have worried about this. I missed holding her. I spent all my free time shopping for her and sending her things. I knew that she would probably grow up loving her grandma more than me, but short of giving up skating, there was nothing I could do about it. That is the life that we chose.

It was the same with me when I was a little girl. I never had a baby-sitter. I didn't know what the word meant. When my mother was away at work for a year, my grandmother was the one who raised me. It's not easy for three generations to all live together in the same house. There were some problems between my father and my grandmother. Just as now, there are sometimes problems with me and Daria and my mom. Sometimes Daria doesn't listen to me because she is listening to my mother. But I have to handle it, because I'd rather Daria be with her grandmother than with a baby-sitter. I'm lucky to have a mother who is so wonderful with my baby, and I think this connection between generations is important. You learn about family history. You learn about responsibility between generations. Already I feel a responsibility for my parents, and it's a nice feeling. It isn't a hardship. How can I be mad that my daughter loves my mother so much, when I remember how much I loved my grandmother? Besides, I love my mom, too.

My mother took Daria back to Moscow in November, though Sergei and I had two days in a hotel with them in New York before they left. I didn't expect Daria to have grown so much, so fast. It was great to see them, but I also knew they were going to go away soon, so I wasn't able to be completely happy. I was also nervous about how Daria would be at home with Veld, our Great Dane. Veld loved my mom very much, and I feared he'd be jealous. But as it turned out, he used to stand by Daria's crib and guard her. I missed Daria every single moment that we toured that fall, but I also knew it was no life for a little baby to be in the hotels, airplanes, and buses.

Later that month we went to Ottawa to visit Marina so she could look at our programs before the professional competitions. She made the *Nut-cracker* a little fresher and teased us that we should begin to train for the 1994 Olympics. She said a lot of professionals were going to compete in Lille-hammer, and she was planting a seed in our heads.

But I was still having trouble with my jumps, so I couldn't take her seriously.

The Landover competition was December 9, and I was very nervous, without much confidence. I thought about Daria all the time, and I kept asking myself, Should I skate or be a mom? This struggle didn't give my mind any rest. But Sergei took my hand to calm me down before we took the ice, and wonder of wonders, I finally landed the double axel that had been giving me so many problems. We defended our professional title just three months after having a baby, which made me proud.

When we flew back to Moscow the next week, I was scared even to hold Daria in my arms, because I thought she would cry right away. But she was fine. We discussed with my mom whether they should come along on the tour next year, but then I had a bad dream. I dreamed I left Daria in a hotel room, and when I got back the housekeeper was yelling at me: "You can't leave babies alone for such a long time!" Very scary. I took that as a sign not to travel with Daria.

We were like gypsies, always living out of hotels and suitcases. Stars on Ice had a Christmas break, and Sergei and I went down to Florida to stay in Brian Orser's parents' condominium in Saint Petersburg. We didn't have anywhere to practice. We were just enjoying the weather. Everywhere else it was winter, and here it was summer.

It was still romantic to be with Sergei, and at

this condominium I could buy food, cook him dinner, light candles—all the things we couldn't do in a hotel. We'd been thinking about buying a house somewhere. If we had a house in the States, my mom could stay there with Daria, and we could at least go visit them when there was a break in the tour. Somewhere closer than Moscow.

Lynn Plage had given us the name of a real estate agent in Tampa, and since we didn't have anything else to do, we started to look at some homes. He started by showing us some very bad places that were cheap. Then he took us to a community in Tampa with a gate and a little lake. There were two day-care centers in this community, and there was a skating rink just twenty minutes away. He showed us a model house that had a girl's room all made up, painted pink, with ballet tutus on the bed. Everything beautiful. And we were thinking it was just perfect for Daria.

The house had three bedrooms, a living room, kitchen, a backyard, and a screened-in pool. All of it tasteful and perfectly arranged. It looked so cute, and we kept saying, "Wouldn't it be great if Daria and Mom were here?" I wanted all my relatives to move into this house. So we asked the man, "Can we have *this* house?"

He said no, that it was the model. But then he said they could build us the exact same house on another lot, and even move the furniture out of the model house and into our new one. The way this real estate agent talked, he just made you buy the house. You had no choice. "Just come tomorrow," he said, "and we'll have the contract for you." So we came the next day, which happened to be Christmas Eve, and signed the contract.

As we were driving away, we both were wondering if what we just did was such a good idea.

But we were so young, and it really didn't feel like a big decision. And we thought we had to buy another car, because this house had a two-car garage. The house was finished in April, just as they said it would be, and Sergei and I came back and lived in it for two or three days. No more. We had to go up to Ottawa and begin working with Marina on our Olympic program. We never moved into this house, and Daria, whom we bought it for, has seen it only once. Like I said, Sergei and I never really planned anything. We seemed to live one day to the next.

Moonlight Sonata

We missed Daria's first Christmas. With sadness and resignation, we sent toys and clothes home to her in Moscow, and we spent New Year's 1993 by ourselves in Dallas, the third straight year we'd been away from home.

I said to Sergei, "Let's do surprises for each other this year. Don't tell me what you're going to get me, and I won't say what I'm going to get you." He agreed to try, although I knew he disliked shopping for me alone.

We went to a mall and picked a spot to meet back at in three hours. I bought some things for him, had them all wrapped, and came back to the appointed place. He was waiting. "All set, Serioche?"

He wasn't all set at all. He asked me to come with him. He wanted to show me what he was thinking of buying, but he didn't know the size, and he wasn't sure if I would like it. Sergei never understood that the surprise was as important as the gift, that his picking something out for me alone, without help, was the best guarantee I would like it. But there was nothing I could do except follow him. It was a warm-up suit from Polo, and he made me try it on before he bought it. So it wasn't a surprise again.

Back in the hotel we waited until midnight to celebrate the New Year. It was just the two of us, and when the time came, we drank champagne and cognac. The hotel had given us a can of Texas black beans that we were supposed to open for luck, which we did. But it was a little sad, because none of our close friends or family were around us. Paul Theofanous had lent me a book of poems by the Russian poet Anna Akhmatova, beautiful love poems, and reading about life in Moscow and Saint Petersburg, knowing that Daria was back there with my mother and father, made me cry.

Life at home had completely changed since our childhood. When the Soviet Union broke up, it was weird, but not a big change for me and Sergei, since we spent so much time traveling in other countries. But for my parents and for Sergei's mother and sister, the change was radical and touched them every day.

Moscow had become crowded with refugees from the warring republics in the south. These people would be huddled in the subway stations, drinking, and smoking marijuana, sometimes begging, sometimes stealing, things we'd never seen when we were young. There was no sense of nostalgia for the old days, but there was a great deal of stress and unrest, which was new.

Moscow was now very wild and open, with Mafia types demanding payment from everyone who opened a business. It was like America when the Mafia ruled during Prohibition. Give the Russians time. All we need is another sixty or seventy years to catch up. *Businessman* was now a word in Russian: *beez-neez-man.* But the rules . . . what rules? It was bizarre. Ladies would go into a store, buy ten bottles of perfume, or five pairs of shoes, then walk out and try to sell these wares on the street for a small markup. Prices were soaring from inflation, making it very difficult for pensioners like Sergei's mother.

In the old days everything was quiet and safe, but there was no progress, no improvement in people's lives. Everyone lived on the same level, but there was no freedom. I personally never felt this lack of freedom, but Sergei did—very much so—because he read more, because he was older, and because he understood more. He knew a lot about Stalin, and he described him to me as someone who wasn't a person, who was unbelievable, so terrible, so wicked. He hated Stalin very much. And although we seldom talked about such things, he also felt badly toward Gorbachev. He didn't hate him, but one time his name came up on television, and Sergei said simply, "He's not a good person. He destroyed Russia, made a good life for himself. He made changes too fast."

It surprised me to hear him say this, because under Gorbachev, our lives—Sergei's and mine—improved, and we could easily go to America to become professional skaters. But Sergei saw it from the eyes of his parents, who couldn't understand this new world with all these new ideas. My grandfather hated Gorbachev, too. That entire generation had spent their lives always listening to their leaders telling them to go straight, go straight, go straight. And now all of a sudden Gorbachev tells them to turn right. He'd be on TV all day long talking about changes, and it made old people angry because they were too old to benefit from these changes, and now they'd be left behind. They worked all their lives for one thing, and now, suddenly, they are told that that thing was wrong. Even if it's better for the young people, it's worse for the old. So Sergei was upset about his parents, who were closer to the old regime than my parents, since they worked for the police. It was like after an entire lifetime of hard work and sacrifice, someone had said to them, "Your revolution, the past seventy years, was worthless."

I don't believe there's a big difference between the Russian people and the American people. Not deep down. Only that Americans know how to work, and Russians are just learning this. In Russia, for many, many years—for many generations, in fact—it wasn't possible to improve your lot in life by working harder. This was true both under the Communists and under the czars. But now this has changed, and in a short time people are learning that to take two jobs is something to be admired. That anyone with energy and brains and a special talent can succeed. They're starting to become workaholics. But they're also starting to find a better life.

Sergei did not quite think this way. He was Russian to his soul, and was only comfortable there. He came to America to work, and he returned to Russia to find peace of mind. He thought the fundamental difference between Americans and Russians was that the Russian culture was so rich, so old, that the people had a very deeply rooted mentality. There was a stolidness, a steadfastness, a stoicism, and a respect for tradition that was uniquely Russian. Americans have a very young culture by comparison. Americans see something that's new, and they love it right away, they use it right away, and they throw it right away, because there's always something coming along to replace it.

❀ ❀ ❀

We hadn't definitely decided whether to compete in the 1994 Olympics yet, but just in case, we were working on our double axels every day, using our practice time to our best advantage. If we decided we wanted to compete, we had to write a letter to the International Skating Union by February 10, asking for amateur reinstatement. Finally we decided to do this.

After touring two months through the eastern United States and Canada, we went to Ottawa in early May to talk to Marina about some ideas for Lillehammer. We decided on a flamenco number for the short program, and she played us Beethoven's *Moonlight* Sonata for the long program, and we liked it right away. She told us she'd been saving this piece of music for us ever since she'd left Russia. Sergei, particularly, liked this number. It was the first time he'd ever responded to a piece of music so strongly.

Marina and Sergei had identical tastes. They were kindred spirits in ways that had always made me a little bit jealous. Maybe more than a little bit, I admit. When Marina worked with us, I thought she became more beautiful, more creative. It was like she was born for us, and we were born for her. She'd choreograph the movements she wanted us to do on the ice, and Sergei would do them perfectly the first time. He knew exactly how she wanted us to move our arms, to hold our heads. Sergei and Marina heard the music exactly the same. I had to learn these things. But I learned.

Marina loved Sergei, I think, which was difficult for me. I treasured working with her, but I was also uncomfortable around her. I didn't particularly like all the time the three of us spent together off the ice, interesting as it was, for Marina was educated in music, ballet, dance history, and art. She was full of stories, and I couldn't help feeling inadequate. At the same time, I realized that Marina was like a gift of God for us, the only one who could create the kind of programs people grew to expect of us, and that Sergei insisted on, because his was always the final word.

We returned to Moscow in mid-May, and once more we were reunited with Daria. One of the things we did in the month we were home was take a complete physical exam from Dr. Viktor Anikanov, who was the speed-skating doctor who had taken care of Sergei at the Calgary Olympics when he came down with a stomach flu. It was a very thorough exam. We got on stationary bicycles, and they gave us each an EKG, where they put nodules on our chests and tested our hearts at rest and during and after strong physical exertion. Dr. Anikanov gave us a clean bill of health. And we had another one of these physicals in the fall.

I think of this often, since two years later Sergei died of coronary heart disease. Two of the arteries to his heart were completely blocked. I have talked to Dr. Anikanov since, and he told me that after Sergei's funeral he went back and rechecked all these tests to see if it were possible he'd missed something. He said there was nothing, not even a tiny clue there was something amiss with Sergei's heart, except that it was slightly enlarged, which is typical of an athlete.

Now I've learned that Sergei was born with a defective gene that was probably responsible for his heart attack.

On June 15 we returned to Ottawa to again work with Marina, this time bringing Mom and Daria. In addition to working on the program, we did ballet classes and a conditioning program created by Marina's husband, Alexei Chetverukhin, whose brother, Sergei, had been a silver medalist in singles in the 1972 Olympics. Alexei was a conditioning expert. We skated about two hours in the morning, then lifted weights and did running. Sprints one day—thirty meters, sixty meters, four hundred meters—and the next day we'd do three laps fast, rest, then three laps fast, rest. That was the killer. Then we'd have another hour of skating in the evening. Sometimes we had time to play tennis, too.

It was very difficult for us to both skate and do off-ice conditioning. Back in the days of the Soviet Union, we never had dry-land training when we were skating. It was one or the other. But we felt we had to speed everything up because Lillehammer was less than eight months away, and I'd missed six full months of training when I had Daria. All our muscles were sore, but it was fun to come home exhausted and watch Daria growing up.

One day she suddenly appeared upstairs. "How did *you* get here, little one?" I said. She had learned to crawl.

Marina told us that since Daria's birth, we had

become more beautiful as pairs skaters, more professional, with a deeper understanding of each other. She said we fit together better, that our lines were cleaner. Performing every night in the shows had taught us how to express our feelings to the audience, to skate the program as a whole, rather than simply going from element to element. "You're doing everything I told you so perfectly. It's almost like you were preparing your whole career for this program," she said one day.

The theme she had created for us with the *Moonlight* Sonata was that of man celebrating woman as the mother of all mankind. She said that Sergei should get on his knees before me, because only the woman can give birth, only the woman can give him his children. Marina, who had studied music at the National Theater Institute in Moscow, said that most composers thought of Beethoven as the foundation of classical music, just as woman was the foundation of mankind. She told us to show the audience how we'd grown as people and as parents since the Calgary Olympics.

The beginning of the program was very soft, and we opened our arms to show the audience and judges that we were opening ourselves up to them. We were showing them not a program, but the story of our life. If you listen to the *Moonlight* Sonata, the music can only represent a man and a woman's life together. It can't mean anything else. It can't mean a season, or a march, or a dance, or a storm, or an animal. It's more, even, than love. *Romeo and Juliet*, that music was about love. But the *Moonlight* Sonata is for older people who have experienced real life. It expresses what changes love can bring about in people, how it can make them stronger, make them have more respect for each other. How it can give them the ability to bring a new life into the world.

In the middle section, the slow section, there was one point where Sergei came and slid to me on his knees, offering me his hands. I put my knees on them, and he then stood on his feet and lifted me. It was quite a difficult lift, because he had to get up from his knees very gracefully. And he didn't hold me there as if I was on a pedestal. Rather, everything was done to movement, and he had to turn around and keep skating. It took a long time to learn this lift, but except for that one element, everything about this program was natural for us. It was easy and comfortable. If Marina told us to do something, it happened. She never said, "You have to show the audience how you love him." She'd say, "How would you hug him if you wanted to tell him you're grateful?" or, "What if you wanted to sit on his knees? How would you do it?" We were just being ourselves on the ice. She wanted us to show everyone how we'd become adults.

During this period, Marina's thirteen-year-old son, Fedor, was training with us. We spent long hours on the ice, and Fedor, who's a promising young singles skater, started complaining to Sergei about it. Sergei, as I mentioned, had his own set of rules, his own code, which he seldom shared with anyone. But he gave some advice to Fedor: (1) If you want to finish well, never hold back on the warm-up; (2) always take yourself to the limit; (3) if you start something, always try to excel at it, or don't begin at all; and (4) don't whine, because it doesn't make practice any shorter.

Sergei lived by these rules, and Fedor, I'm certain, will never forget them.

Training in the New Russia

*I*n early August we went back to Moscow, and one of the first things we did was to visit our friends Sergei Ponomarenko and Marina Klimova. We brought some cake with us to their three-room apartment, which was much larger than ours. We kept telling them they should have kids to help them fill up all that space. "No, we should work," they said. "Soon, soon." But how soon no one knows.

We wanted to ask their advice about whether to pay any money to the president of the Russian ice skating federation, Valentin Piseev. We were thinking maybe a couple of thousand dollars, and even had this money in an envelope. We were worried that if we didn't do something like that, Piseev might declare one of our lifts illegal at the Nationals, and suddenly our Olympic dream would be finished. He was also in charge of doling out ice time for practice. That's the way business was being done in Russia then, and Marina Zueva also thought we should give some money to Piseev.

Sergei Ponomarenko only said it would be a nice gesture, not a bad idea, and that Piseev would certainly like it. He didn't tell us if two years earlier, before Albertville, they had given Piseev money. He didn't say it was absolutely necessary to do it. He only said that Piseev would appreciate it. Ponomarenko added that he didn't think it was necessary to do it right away; it would soon become clear if this bribe was essential or not.

We left without making a decision, but as it turned out we never made the payment. We realized we were quite important to the federation, even without the money. Piseev did ask us to do him a favor, which was to skate in a couple of exhibitions in the town of Arkhangelsk, and we were only too happy to do it.

We were training at the army club, and we asked our old coach, Vladimir Zaharov, the man who had put us together, to keep an eye on our skating and correct us if something was wrong. We had long since normalized relations with him since he'd refused to coach us after Sergei, age sixteen, had missed too many practices. For years we had trained on the same ice as he and his young students. We couldn't very well not talk to one another. So now, Zaharov watched us every

day, and he helped us, too. Little things, he
noticed, like Sergei's knees had to be more bent
on the death spiral, or we needed more speed, or
our arms weren't parallel when they should be.
Things we couldn't see by ourselves. He was very
good.

Vladislav Kostin from the Bolshoi theater made
our costumes again, and for the *Moonlight* Sonata
he came up with navy-blue velvet with white pip-
ing around the collar and down the front—very
stark, very simple, almost like priests' robes.
Marina wasn't sure that these costumes fit the
program's theme: mother as foundation of
mankind. It was not a bad point. She suggested
maybe a light gray and yellow costume for me, as
if I was the moonlight, and something very dark
for Sergei, as if he was the night. But Vladislav
said absolutely no, he couldn't imagine any other
color for Beethoven than navy blue. He was quite
intractable on this point. He said to try it for one
competition and then decide.

So we did. Our first pre-Olympic competition
was Skate Canada, in Ottawa, which we wanted
to do first because Marina lived there, and also
because our first international competition ever
was Skate Canada, in 1985, and we thought it
might bring us luck. Piseev's federation wasn't
happy about this decision because they thought
that with Isabelle Brasseur and Lloyd Eisler being
from Canada, the judges might put them first. As
it turned out, Brasseur and Eisler weren't even in

Training at the Army Club before the 1994 Olympics with (left to right) *Leonovich, Zueva, and Zaharov.*

the competition. We skated very well and we won, the only problem arising when, during the short program, I caught a thread from my costume on Sergei's button, and it unraveled, so I had this huge black thing trailing after me. We were also quite surprised how much money they were now paying to amateurs: we got three thousand dollars for the event.

That fall Sergei's sister's boyfriend, Dmitri, died. That dear woman has had much tragedy in her life. Dmitri was in his late thirties, no more, and Natalia had loved him for two years. He died in her arms of a heart attack.

Sergei and I went to Dmitri's funeral, and Sergei was holding Natalia all the time, squeezing her hands. She's very strong, and wasn't crazy or crying with grief, but she looked almost gray in color. Some members of Dmitri's family were bothering her, saying Dmitri had owed them money and asking her to pay his debts. Such terrible things. I don't know how people can act this way in the face of another's misery. Sergei was so tender and compassionate with his sister, whom he loved so. He called her not Natalia, but Natooshik. At their home following the funeral, he said to her, "Natooshik, Dmitri's all around us. He's not in human form, but he's in this kitchen right now; he's in this bedroom. He can see you and hear you, even if you can't see him." It was very helpful to her, and made her feel so much better. I had never heard Sergei talk this way before, and when Natalia reminded me of this after Sergei had died, it made me feel better, too.

*   *   *

We went to Navagorsk to get ready for the Nationals. The competition was very important, since if we performed badly, we would not be invited to represent Russia in the Olympics. We had heard that the Saint Petersburg pair of Artur Dmitriev and Natalia Mishkutenok, gold medalists in 1992, were skating very well, and we knew they'd be our toughest competition.

At Navagorsk, they were now charging money to the athletes who trained there. Also, athletes from other countries were using the facilities—Finnish soccer players, Ukrainian volleyball players. No longer was the Russian government expending its limited resources on the country's elite athletes. Administrators of sports facilities had to figure out ways for them to support themselves, and charging room and board was one solution. It was just one of the many changes

St. Petersburg during the 1994 Nationals.

since the breakup of the Soviet Union. The hotel at Navagorsk was still quite clean, but the food wasn't as good as it had been. No caviar anymore. Fortunately for the skaters, the head coach of CSKA, Elena Chaikovskaya, had found a commercial sponsor, a Russian company called Anis, which was picking up the tab for our expenses.

It was much harder to get into competitive shape that year than it had ever been for me before. Much harder than I'd ever imagined. Sergei pushed me and pushed me, whereas when we'd been younger, I was the one trying to push him. He got me to go to the gym. We skated twice a day, in the morning and evening, and he worked hard with me to get my double axel, my nemesis jump, perfect.

Sergei had never given me skating advice before, so I was excited to listen to him. And he always had good tips. Sergei would have been an excellent coach. You don't just tell a skater that she should be jumping higher. You say, You have to use this arm when you jump. You have to have your body positioned exactly so. If I said we should try something again, in years past he'd have responded, "It's okay, Katuuh, we'll leave it for tomorrow." But this year he'd stay out on the ice with me as long as I wanted.

And, of course, the other difficult thing was spending so much time away from Daria. She never came with us to Navagorsk, and we didn't even have a crib for her in our little Moscow apartment. When she was with us, we just pushed two armchairs together for her to sleep on, and that was fine. But usually she stayed with my mom, and we tried to visit her every day.

So it was tough—mentally, physically, emotionally. But whatever sacrifices were involved in getting ready for the 1994 Lillehammer Games, I was willing to make them. It was only for a short while, and this Olympics was going to be different from the first one. One of the reasons I wanted to go to another Olympics was I didn't remember half of what happened in Calgary. It was almost like I'd been blind to everything but the skating. I'd been sixteen, and everything was too easy for me. The Olympics was just another competition.

Not this time. I was determined to remember all the faces, all the people, all the experiences, all the feelings—whether we won or lost. I would try to take everything inside me and hold it there, so I could call upon it forever.

Sergei and I won at the Nationals in December, skating well except when I two-footed my double axel in the *Moonlight* Sonata program. Everyone loved the program, though. It was the first time we'd won the Nationals since 1987, which in truth was a harder competition for us than either the Europeans or the Worlds, because of all the young and hungry pairs teams who compete in Russia.

That year we celebrated the new year at home, in my parents' apartment, and I bought fresh mussels for us to eat. The last time Sergei and I had been there for the New Year's festivities was in 1988, which also boded well for our luck. I remembered very well that night six years earlier, when Sergei shyly came to our party, and I gave him the needlepoint I'd done of the clown. That was the first year we'd broken the plate at midnight, and I'd grabbed a piece and hidden it somewhere very safe and I made a wish that I would skate well in Calgary. That truly seemed like a lifetime ago. We forgot this tradition of breaking the plate, however, and at the stroke of midnight, Sergei and I were debating whether or not to wake Daria. We decided not to. We didn't stay up very late that night to welcome in 1994, because we had to go to Garmisch-Partenkirchen the next day for the annual New Year's show.

That was the first time we saw Oksana Baiul. She was coached by Galina Zmievskaya, which was surprising to us, because Galina never trained girls. I remember Galina telling me the year before about Oksana, when she was just fourteen, and I thought to myself, for Galina to brag about this girl no one's ever heard of, she must really be good. A short time later, in her very first appearance there, she won the 1993 World Championship.

Oksana was so young. Galina's daughter, Nina Petrenko, who was married to Viktor, kept following her around during the Garmisch exhibition because Oksana didn't know where her dress was, where her hairpiece was, what time she was supposed to go on. She couldn't take care of herself. I dressed beside her before the exhibition, and she wasn't a bit timid or shy. German television had prepared a special feature on Oksana. In the dressing room, this program was playing on the TV, but she didn't seem to want to watch it at all. We were all warming up for the show, doing our stretching exercises, and Oksana was looking around, eating something. Nina Petrenko said she never warmed up before skating.

It was strange, but I felt kind of proud to be with this girl. When I was first in the Olympics, I was the same age as Oksana was when I first met her, and just being around her made me feel younger. She wasn't in the least bit awed to talk to the older, more experienced skaters. I needed a barrette for my hair, and she casually said, "Here you go," and tossed me one. Then I watched her do her number, to *Swan Lake*, and it was very beautiful. Her dress was so professional, and so was her hairpiece, and she did not skate at all like a young girl. Everything was as it was supposed to be.

The European Championships in 1994 were in Copenhagen, which was also a good sign for Sergei and me, since they'd also been there in 1986, the first year that we won the Worlds. We stayed in the same hotel, used the same dressing room, walked down the same streets. We went to the same store to shop and drew our starting order from the same hall. Each time I discovered something the same, I mentioned it to Sergei, who told me that I talked too much about the past. He said it was a very bad habit.

It was great to see everybody again, all the professionals who had come back to the amateur ranks. We saw Katarina Witt getting ready, and she said to us, "It's a different life now, right?" She was laughing and having fun and appeared relaxed, but I didn't believe it. I think that was all put on for show.

We, on the other hand, were not at all relaxed. We were as serious and intense as we'd ever been, spurred on by a fear of failure. The day before the short program we had an 8:00 A.M. practice, and we were the only skaters who showed up. That's when I thought we were really crazy. But Sergei had been focused like that all year. I was amazed at how intent he was on getting us ready. It had started way back the previous March and April, during the Stars on Ice tour, when we only had a half hour of practice ice a day. He'd say, "This practice we have to pay more attention to the triple twist." The next practice, it would be our spins. Something different every day, and always very specific.

As a result, I felt absolutely confident and comfortable with both our long and short programs, and I think the European Championships was the best that we skated them, better even than the Olympics. We beat Dmitriev and Mishkutenok, as we'd done at the Nationals, which also gave us confidence. Ice dancers Jayne Torvill and Christopher Dean had also returned to amateur competition that year, and in Copenhagen they drew big audiences to all of their practices. They skated great, and also won the Europeans, but I liked the Russian team of Oksana Gritschuk and Evgeny Platov better. Torvill and Dean were almost too perfect, too professional. Their program didn't bring any excitement. In the women's competition, Oksana was beaten by Surya Bonaly of France.

In America the big news was this attack on Nancy Kerrigan in which Tonya Harding was involved. We didn't hear much about it in Russia, but Marina told us that every day at home they were leading the newscasts with it. The attack was almost beyond my comprehension—dirty, inhuman—and left a black mark on the whole sport. I always believed sport was supposed to bring people together, to bring them peace as well as great entertainment. The whole world watches the Olympic Games, waiting for them every four years. It is one of the things that is beautiful on this earth, and to have them spoiled by something so unsportsmanlike was terribly sad.

Everywhere there was also a lot of talk about how the professional skaters had returned to amateur competition and were closing the door on the younger athletes. The whole year they kept asking us about this in the press. I hated this conversation. It's sport. We weren't closing any doors. All of us were on the same road, competing under the same rules.

It was a very exciting and uncertain time in figure skating, for ridiculous reasons and fine ones.

Lillehammer

$\mathscr{B}$efore we left for Lillehammer, Sergei and I went to talk to Father Nikolai. I had been doing this before all our competitions, but this was the first time that Sergei had come. I didn't push him. I just said, "I want to see Nikolai, do you want to come with me?"

What I liked about talking to Father Nikolai was that you never had to bring words or questions with you. Father Nikolai always found something to say. This time he said, "I just want to tell you I'm going to pray that God gives you strength to get through the competition, and that you should thank God for giving you the chance to go. You should thank Him for giving you something you both love to do, together. I can't pray for you to win. You have to look to each other for this. You can't ask God to please help you win. Better to ask that He give you a chance to be happy when you skate. And remember your Daria, that you're skating for her. And remember your parents, too."

It was very enlightening for us. When you train as hard as we'd been training, when you're as focused on a goal as we'd been, you sometimes forget the people around you. You even forget there's a world around you, because you're thinking about the gold medal all the time. Father Nikolai was reminding us that God doesn't care about gold medals, that the very idea of beating someone in competition doesn't go very well with religious thinking. His reminder to remember my family helped me, just as this thought had helped me in my first Olympics at Calgary.

Sergei and I said goodbye to our parents, goodbye to Daria, and flew to Oslo with the rest of the team. I had to smile when they passed out our team uniforms—dark purple and white, not at all tasteful—since these ugly outfits didn't fit me any better than they had six years earlier in Calgary. The boots for the opening ceremonies came up over my knees. Only huge women should compete for Russia in the Olympics.

We took a bus to Hamar, a town near Lillehammer, where the skating competitions were held. There was so much snow, everything pristine and white. The town where we were staying looked like a village. I liked it right away. I liked the little sleds that the women pushed along the icy streets, holding their groceries. Some women walked their

Sergei, in Lillehammer, at the opening procession.

dogs this way, tying the leash to the handle of the sled. I liked the way the people all wore the same red, white, and blue sweaters. They were so friendly and welcoming to us. It felt like a real celebration of winter.

The pairs skaters were always the first team members to arrive, so Sergei and I were allowed to move into the nicest room. We were staying in a wood house with a living room, four bedrooms, two bathrooms, and even a washer and dryer. It was more like a winter weekend cottage than an Olympic Village. Two of the rooms had double beds, so Sergei and I took one of those. Ice dancers Maia Usova and Alexander Zhulin, who were married at the time—they've since divorced—had the other double room. And the two single rooms were taken by our chief competition, Artur Dmitriev and Natalia Mishkutenok.

We were friendly with them, however. Artur and Sergei were particularly good friends. Artur is a very funny storyteller, and he likes to tell tales about his army days, which Sergei never believed. Artur is very big and strong, and his stories always seemed to involve him lifting huge objects. Sergei would shake his head and say something like, "Here we go again, Artur the superman." They were always kidding each other in the manner of men. Artur is married to a famous rhythmic gymnast, and on tours he was always the first person to host room parties. He liked very much to entertain. And of course he's a very creative and artistic

skater, frequently adding little embellishments to
his program on the spur of the moment.

Natalia was much more quiet, more reserved.
She never talked, even in dressing rooms or at
parties. We weren't close friends, but we never
had any bad feelings toward each other, and I
think we respected each other's skating. I remember she loved to go very fast, whether in cars or
on snow skis. She was a terrific skier. She also
worked out all the time in the gym, because it
was difficult for her to keep her weight down.
She tried hard, but this was always a problem.

I was more nervous before the short program
than I ever remember being in my life. Far more
nervous than I'd been in Calgary. In the morning
practice, I hadn't skated well, and then I had the
rest of the day to think about it. All the time I was
looking at Sergei.

He was, as ever, so calm. I just smiled at him
every once in a while, and he could see in my smile
how nervous I was, so he kept holding my hand.
All afternoon, I kept thanking God I had someone
to hold onto. It feels so much more secure when
you're holding your partner's hand. Marina had
told me not to worry, that I'd be fine. And I kept
telling myself I should relax, I shouldn't be so serious. By the evening, when it was time to skate, I'd
at last started to calm down.

Like all the returning professionals, we were
skating early in the draw. The seedings were
always done according to the previous World

Championships. Knowing that Daria and my parents were watching on television was a big comfort to me. When you first skate onto the ice and see all those blinding, bright lights, all those people who are too far away to make eye contact with, you can't help feeling scared of them. It's weird. You feel as though there are thousands of eyes on you waiting to see what you can or can't do. At least I always felt that way, especially in Lillehammer, where it was a huge building and the spectators were high above us and seemingly quite far away.

I remember thinking that the fans were primarily there to see an interesting competition, something unusual, out of the ordinary—to see which pair would miss the critical element. This was sport, right? It wasn't like one of the exhibition tours, where the audience is just there to enjoy the music, the costumes, and everyone's skating. This was the Olympics, and the fans all had their own favorites. Rightly or wrongly, I was afraid that for most people sitting out there, we were not their favorites.

That's why Father Nikolai's reminder about remembering Daria and my parents, who were watching at home, was such a comfort. It brought me back into myself. It shielded me from these crazy thoughts racing through me, calmed me, and gave me a focus. And always, the last thing going through my head before taking the ice was something Marina had said: Forget about everyone else. Skate for Sergei.

So I did, and in the short program, our flamenco number, we made it through without any mistakes. We finished a little bit early, just ahead of the music, but we always skated faster in the competition than we did in practice because of the adrenaline. Sergei, who had to consciously shorten his strides so they matched mine in length, sometimes complained that he couldn't keep up.

Afterwards we watched Natalia and Artur, and they were very good. Artur was so excited when he finished that when he got down on his knee for his final pose, he fell. But he improvised something to make it look okay, as only Artur could do. At the end of the night, we were scored first, with Artur and Natalia in second.

That night we didn't talk at the house about skating, except to mention the positions we drew for the final. We were the third to skate in the final grouping, and Artur and Natalia were just before us. I didn't like to skate third. I always preferred the second spot, because you can have a good warm-up, take a short rest, then skate. When you're third, you're already cooled off before the time comes to skate. Also, I can't stand for fifteen minutes in my skates when they're laced up. Sergei could, but not me. So I'd have to untie them, then do them up again.

The next day, the day of the long program, I had a good appetite, which surprised me. Sergei, on the other hand, didn't have an appetite, which was very unusual for him. He hadn't slept well, either.

It was the most nervous I'd ever seen him, although he didn't say anything about it.

We always went for some sort of walk before a competition, so at about five o'clock we went to look at a cute little church. They were preparing it for a concert of some kind. I don't remember what we talked about. Probably nothing. When I was nervous before a competition, the important thing was always just to get outside. If I stayed indoors, I felt as if I couldn't get enough air to breathe. I'd be in the arena, going here and there, trying to find a good spot to stand, and it wasn't until I stepped outside that I suddenly felt better, felt I could fill my lungs with air.

Later, we went through our usual stretching and off-ice warm-ups. But I didn't say very much to Sergei while we waited to skate. Sergei was in the men's dressing room, and I was in the ladies' dressing room putting on my makeup. I do remember asking him to tell Marina not to hover. She had this habit of hovering over me as I prepared, coming up to me all the time and asking if I needed help. Sergei must have said something to her, too, because this time she refrained.

The warm-up on the ice is the worst. You can't really feel your legs yet. You have to watch out for the other skaters, and also watch the time on the clock. Even when you see the time, you're so nervous you don't know what it means. The warm-up lasts six minutes, the clock reads five minutes, and you wonder, Five minutes have gone, or five minutes remain? Your mind is a blank, and all you know is which elements are still left to try.

Then you must get off the ice and wait. Isabelle Brasseur and Lloyd Eisler were the first to skate the long program, then Natalia and Artur. Sergei still had his boots laced up; mine were untied. I was looking at a picture of Daria, whom we called Dasha, and trying to think of my parents, as Father Nikolai had advised. Marina came up and told us that Lloyd Eisler and Isabelle Brasseur skated perfectly. Then, a little later, she reported that Natalia and Artur, too, were perfect. I don't know why she kept telling us these things. As we headed out to the ice, I could see that Tamara

Heinz Kluetmeier

*In the "kiss and cry" area before winning
our second Olympic gold medal.*

Moskvina, the coach of Natalia and Artur, was happy, and I tried to listen to their marks when they were announced, reminding myself, Katia, don't forget, you wanted to remember everything about these Olympics.

The spectators were still settling back down in their seats after giving Natalia and Artur a standing ovation. The hall finally quieted, and I could feel that everyone was waiting for us to do something very special. It was an intimidating feeling. So I tried to forget about the audience. You can go crazy if you think about them too much. You'll melt out there. Even if people want to help you, they can't. Very seldom does this crowd bring you energy.

I've always said that the Olympics are a celebration of nerves, and never are they more on edge than in the moments before you begin, when every eye is on you, every light is on you. Before I came out on the ice, I'd been thinking about Daria and my parents. But now that I was out there, all I thought about was Sergei. We must skate for each other. I've wanted this for such a long time, and now we're here. He's probably so nervous, but I looked at him and thought, No, he's strong and calm like always. He's okay.

And suddenly, all the nervousness went away. Finally, with nothing left to wait for, I asked my body, Please, do what you can do. We took our pose at the center of the ice, waiting for the opening notes of the *Moonlight* Sonata, and I happened to be looking toward the "kiss and cry" area. I saw

Natalia and Artur stand up to go after their marks had been read, and I saw them hug Tamara. And I was thinking: You're alert, Katia. You're very aware of everything going on around you. They're finished, and now it is our turn to skate. And all of a sudden, the music was already playing.

It's nice when you're thinking when you skate, when you're not just doing things automatically, like a robot. It's nice for the audience, too. I enjoyed skating the *Moonlight* Sonata in Lillehammer. I remember everything. You cannot describe these four minutes of skating in words, but I was aware of every movement that I was making, conscious of the meaning behind these movements and conscious of what Sergei was doing. It is a clarity that one so seldom finds elsewhere in life, a clarity any athlete can relate to, moments in time that we remember the rest of our lives. I believe it is why we compete.

I was not sure, however, if Sergei made a single or double salchow. Something seemed wrong, and afterward, as we were hugging each other, I asked him. He never liked to tell me bad things, so he didn't answer. Then I asked him more simply. "Double?" He shook his head. It was the first mistake I could remember him ever making. He was very upset, but unless you knew him well, you wouldn't have known.

Marina was with us in the kiss and cry area, and before the scores went up, she told us everything was all right. Her eyes were bright red, which is what always happened when she tried to control her emotions. After the scores were recorded, no one told us right away that we'd won. It was close, but eight of the nine judges scored us first. Then Tracy Wilson, my roommate from our first North American tour, did an interview with us for CBS, and when she congratulated us, we finally knew.

The first thing I thought of as we stood on the podium listening to the Russian anthem play, watching the Russian flag be raised, was, It's over now. It's what you wanted, and now it's over.

I was proud of myself for skating clean, landing both double axels after struggling with them for the last three years. Sergei, I could see, wasn't happy. Gold medal or not, he was not used to making mistakes. Still, his many friends on the speed-skating team brought a smile to his lips as they screamed for him as we accepted our medals. I thought the audience clapped more for Artur and Natalia than for us, which upset me a little bit.

But there were certainly no hard feelings between us, and we went back to the house and celebrated together for the next three days. Artur knew he and Natalia had skated their best, and Sergei was the type of man who could beat you but afterward you still wanted to go have a beer with him. He and Artur talked all the time the rest of the Olympics, and because they're friends, they could share their opinions about each other, and their skating, very easily. Natalia and I weren't like this. But we did go skiing together three times in Lillehammer. It was only my third time on snow skis, and I started at the very, very small hill, like the little kids. Then I went with Natalia and Sergei to the bigger hill, and Natalia, who loves speed, left me because I was falling down so often. Sergei was waiting for me all the time. "Serioque? Are you down there? I'm coming." It was fun.

The day after we won, we were invited to a party at the Russia House, a hospitality center for Russian visitors in Lillehammer, to celebrate. We were driving with Evgenia Shishkova and Vadim Naumov, the Russian pairs team who had finished fourth, and a month later won the World Championships. Naumov said to Sergei, "So, what was the reason you came back? Just to win another gold medal? You didn't improve. We could have won the bronze if you'd stayed professional."

Sergei didn't say anything in return. What can you say to a person with such a mentality? We have an expression in Russia: After the fighting is over, don't swing your fists.

We originally thought we would also go on to the World Championships in Chiba, Japan, but we were so relaxed after the Olymics, we decided not to. This gold medal in 1994 satisfied me in a way no other medal I'd won ever had, even though we had made this one mistake. I knew how hard we'd worked and how well we'd skated the whole year. I knew how much we'd sacrificed personally, spending that time away from Daria. And I was satisfied it had been worth it. The first gold medal we had won for the Soviet Union. This one we won for each other.

Simsbury and
a New Home

Shortly after the Olympics, *People* magazine
took a picture of me for their issue naming the "50
Most Beautiful People in the World." I didn't like
it when someone asked me to be in a photo shoot,
and not Sergei. I always thought, we're a pair. We
should be together in the magazines. But that didn't
stop me from modeling for *People* for five hours. I
asked Sergei if he wanted to come along to watch,
but he told me to go ahead by myself. The photog-
rapher had rented a suite at the Metropole in
Moscow for the shoot, the same suite that Michael
Jackson stayed in when he visited the city. It even
had a sauna in it. We changed dresses, chose costumes, put on jewelry, took off jewelry, carried
skates, took off skates. I did my own makeup. It
was fun.

I didn't realize how big a deal it was until the

issue came out. We were on tour in the United States with Tom Collins's World and Olympic champions, and I remember being so proud until Marina Klimova showed me the magazine and said, "They made a bad picture of you."

"Maybe next time they'll do a better job," I said.

Then I showed the magazine to Sergei and asked him if he liked it.

He said, "Oh, it's nice. But it's not with me."

Now I started to get upset about it. Lynn Plage gave me a big framed picture of the magazine photo, but by then I couldn't look at it without feeling badly, so I sent it to Moscow. My parents still have this picture hanging in their apartment, so at least my mom and dad appreciated it.

There were thirteen Russians on Tommy's tour that spring, more than ever before, which was great fun for us. We performed in sixty-five cities, and during the last month Daria and my mom traveled with us. For some reason, Daria was afraid of all men. As soon as she'd see Tom, she'd start to cry. But besides that, she was a good little traveler.

Tom wanted to give us a contract for the next three years, but he said he would have to pay us less per show than he was paying us now. I talked to Jay Ogden at IMG, and he offered us a four-year deal for a little more money to skate in Stars on Ice. It wasn't as much as we'd heard some of the other gold medalists were making, or even as much as some silver medalists, if they were American. Russian skaters, we'd been told, were never paid the same as North Americans. But I didn't think I could ask Oksana or Viktor or Scott—even the closest friends—how much they were making. I just couldn't. All the time, we were thinking that we're being taken advantage of by the agents. They knew much more than we did, and they spoke their own language. Not only the English language, which is how the contracts were written, but the legal language. It gives me a headache to even look at these contracts. But what could we do? We ended up signing for what Jay suggested, and were happy with it. There was nothing in our background to prepare Sergei and me for contract negotiations.

While we were on this tour, Bob Young came and talked to us about training in the new facility that he was managing in Simsbury, Connecticut. We'd seen Bob a few times with the American teams, coaching pairs, and he told us that Viktor, Oksana, and Galina Zmievskaya were all moving to Simsbury to train at this International Skating Center.

Ever since Daria was born, we knew that if we were going to make a living as professional skaters, we'd have to move to the United States. There was nowhere for us to work in Russia. We could coach there, but for what salary? To get a five-room apartment in Moscow, which we'd looked into, cost as much as our house in Florida, and certainly not less than a hundred thousand dollars. We told Bob Young to talk to Jay Ogden about it, and Jay made a deal with him that in return for doing two shows a year at this new facility, we could have a free condominium in Simsbury to live in, and free ice time. It made much more sense for us to do this, and live near other Russian friends, than to move to the home we'd bought in Tampa.

In mid-August we decided to visit this Simsbury facility and see what this condominium looked like. We told our parents that we were going, but we didn't know where we were going. We weren't thinking of it as a permanent move. We flew to New York, drove the two hours to Simsbury, and when we saw the condominium Bob had arranged for us, we fell in love with it right away. We liked the nearness to New York and the small-town feeling of Simsbury. Debbie Nast, who worked with Jay at IMG, had gotten us a bed, a coffee maker, towels, and sheets. Bob gave us a television and telephone. And those were the only pieces of furniture we had in this condominium for the first six months. It felt like a place for a honeymoon, for making a little nest.

Then Bob took us to see the place where the rink was to be built. They hadn't even poured the cement yet. It was just sand and boards. He showed us the plans, but we were laughing, figuring we wouldn't be staying in this great condominium for long. It was just a wonderful dream. The way they build buildings in Moscow, we were sure it would be another five years before Simsbury had its training center.

But by October it was finished. My mom came over with Daria, and for the first time in our lives, Sergei and I felt like we had our own home. Daria had a bedroom of her own, which Sergei had wallpapered by himself as a surprise to both of us.

He set up her bed and hung the pictures and mirror on the wall, all of it very professionally. It was the first time he'd ever done anything like that with his hands, and he enjoyed it. He was good at it. Sergei generally believed that if you were going to do something, you might as well excel at it or not get started at all. His father had been quite a carpenter. He had built their dacha outside Moscow by himself, driving up every weekend to work on this dacha alone. It gave me reason to think maybe someday Sergei would build a house for me.

* * *

That summer Marina created a new program for us which we began to refer to as "the Rodin number." This was my favorite exhibition program. Every night it was like a new story to tell.

It was set to the music of Rachmaninoff, who was one of Marina's favorite composers, and the program was based on the sculptures of Auguste Rodin. I don't know where Marina got this idea, but she gave us a book of Rodin's sculptures, which we'd bring to the ice rink. Then Sergei and I would try to copy some of the poses in the book.

It was unbelievably difficult, because most of the sculptures were of people in fantastic positions. They weren't merely standing. Some looked as if they were weightlessly reaching out in the sky, and we had to try to reenact these poses while skating. It was all new, different, hard, but also quite interesting. We tried even to mimic the way he had sculpted a pair of hands, intertwined. In one part I had to come around the back of Sergei, which I'd never done before on the ice. He was always the one holding me in front of him. At the end of the program, Sergei lay on the ice, pulled his knees up, and I lay on his knees on my back. Then I threw my head back to look into his eyes.

All the poses were about love, pure and unspoiled. The idea of this program was to show

how love is beautiful, how a man and woman's body are beautiful. For costumes, we first considered tan bodysuits, so we'd look like nude statues,

In the Rodin Museum in Paris with the statue that inspired my favorite program.

because many of Rodin's sculptures are erotic. Not pornographic, but erotic in a natural way. But we settled on a very simple, wraparound skirt for me, tan colored, and rust-colored pants and T-shirt for Sergei. They showed the beauty of the body and the beauty of the forms we were making on the ice. Essentially, we were skating as moving artworks.

Marina wanted this number to be entitled "The Kiss," because that was the name of her favorite sculpture, and the one we posed as at the beginning. We didn't actually kiss, but we almost did. What I found magical about this program was that every time we skated it, it was different. One day I could touch Sergei here, touch him there; the next day I could touch him someplace different. Marina only said to me, "In this part, make him warm." She said to Sergei, "Feel her touch. Show us that you feel it."

I never got tired of skating this program. Although it was too difficult to be sensual for us, we continued to get new feelings from it throughout the year, and we continued to improve it. We started working on it in August 1994, and I think we skated our best performance in April 1995. Every night I heard the music as if for the first time. That was the magic.

*   *   *

My grandfather, Diaka, died in September 1994. I still think of this gentle man whenever I see mushrooms growing in the wild, and I hope I am able to teach Daria the things he taught me. Soon after this, on my mother's birthday, Veld, our Great Dane, also died. Our string of bad luck had begun.

Sergei and I traveled so much that fall that we never even had a week in our condominium. Always, another exhibition or competition. But it was great to feel we could come back to our own house, to go to work then return and see our baby. We couldn't wish for anything better.

We spent a month in Lake Placid in the fall rehearsing for that year's Stars on Ice, but this time Debbie Nast helped get us a condominium. So Daria and Mom were also with us. The whole cast, which we thought of as our extended family, got together for a big Thanksgiving dinner, which is a holiday we don't have in Russia. We don't have turkey in Russia, or sweet potatoes, or cranberry sauce—my favorite—so for us this Thanksgiving dinner was fairly exotic.

The closest thing we have to a Russian Thanksgiving is in February, the middle of winter, when we celebrate something called Butter Holiday, just prior to a religious fast. It's a week-long holiday in which the purpose, like Thanksgiving, is to eat as much as you can. On Butter Holiday, though, Russians serve blini, which are Russian pancakes. They fill them with caviar, or sausage, or sour cream, then fill them with jam for dessert. Unfortunately, I don't particularly like to eat blini, so this is not one of my favorite feasts.

In December, Sergei and I won the World Professional Championships for the third time, skating a Gershwin program as our technical number and the Rodin number as our artistic one. My mother went home to celebrate Christmas with my father and sister, and Daria stayed with us in

Simsbury. The tour opened in Boston Garden on December 27, and we had no choice but to bring Daria to the rehearsal there the day before. Debbie

Irene Ersek

Skating to Gershwin's "Crazy for You."

Heinz Kluetmeier

With the cast of Stars on Ice.

said she'd watch Daria for us. But dear Dasha, who was two, was scared of Debbie. It was terrible. Every time we tried to rehearse something, she started screaming. Debbie was so distraught. She kept saying, I came to help you, and I can't. We'd put Dasha down in a chair beside the ice and tell her, "Look, Mommy and Daddy are going to skate right there. You sit and watch, okay?" But as soon as the music started again, she'd begin screaming like someone was torturing her. Sandra Bezic, the director of the show, tried to calm her. Michael Seibert, Sandra's associate choreographer, tried to calm her. But nothing worked. Sergei finally had to lift her in his arms and skate with her the whole rehearsal.

After that ordeal we called my mother in Moscow. Mom? How was your Christmas? When are you coming back? Not tomorrow? Why not? Here's a ticket we bought for you.

Peter Bregg

On the Stars on Ice tour bus.

The tour—forty-seven cities from Portland, Oregon, to Portland, Maine, over the next three months—was great fun. The luggage traveled everywhere by bus, and we had our choice of whether to go with the luggage or fly. The bus rides themselves were quite comfortable. The driver always had homemade soup for us, and there was a refrigerator stocked with cold beer, a coffee maker, two televisions, and a dozen or so sleeping bunks. For the first time there were four other Russians in Stars on Ice, Elena Bechke and Denis Petrov and ice dancers Natalia Annenko and Genrikh Sretenski. The six of us usually sat together in one of the booths in the back, which the North American skaters started calling the Russia Room. Kurt Browning and Scott Hamilton used to come back and ask, "Can I have a seat in the Russia Room, please?" Kurt, in fact, gave us a poster of the Russian Tea Room in New York to hang on the wall back there.

A lot of the arenas we skated in were ones we'd performed in before, and what amazed me was that Sergei remembered everybody. We'd be standing beside the ice, and he'd say, "That's the same Zamboni driver as last year." Or he'd remember the dressing room attendants or the security guards. Sometimes even individual fans. For me, I don't even see these people. But Sergei was the absolute opposite of a snob. In fact, I think he'd have preferred to spend an evening with these people than in the company, even, of skaters.

What he disliked were the receptions afterward, when the fancy people would come up and whisper, so the other skaters wouldn't hear, "I think you were the best." Sergei hated flattery. That was the worst for him.

This tour finally ended in April. Back home in Simsbury, we were so exhausted from the season that all we wanted to do was relax. It was spring,

At home in Simsbury with our neighbors
Vladimir and Victor Petrenko.

and all the flowers were out. We sat out on the porch and had long breakfasts every day, and Sergei would feed bread to the squirrels. It was so nice not to rush, not to have to put anything in a suitcase. We didn't watch anything. We watched only each other, and Daria.

We had one more exhibition in Lausanne, Switzerland. The weather was beautiful, and Sergei and I walked around town holding hands. It was a weekday, yet all the people were walking outside, enjoying the sunshine. It looked like a Sunday. We talked about how great that was, how these people didn't live to work. How they hadn't forgotten they had just one life to live. You go to Europe, and your eyes just relax from the beauty around you, and you see the people having wine with their lunch in the sun, and you wonder, Is every day here a holiday? In America, people go to the gym instead of having lunch.

We talked about how the villages in Russia, like the one where Yegor lived on the Volga River, were also like this. If it's a nice day, maybe the people skip work. They don't care that it's a day they don't put another dollar in their pocket. And this was Sergei's nature, too.

The Last Summer

For my twenty-fourth birthday Sergei drove me to New York—to drive in a car with Sergei was still my favorite thing to do—and he bought me a Louis Vuitton handbag. Then, just when I thought it was another year without a surprise, the next morning he made me breakfast in bed.

This was my dream. I had mentioned it to Lynn Plage when she asked me for the Stars on Ice program what my perfect day would be. I told her it would begin with Sergei making me breakfast in bed. This was quite a fantasy, since Sergei didn't even know how to make coffee. But Scott Hamilton found out from Lynn what I had said, and he made Sergei promise to fulfill my dream. Scott told me that Sergei had given him this promise, so I began to tease him a little.

"Serioque, are you going to make me breakfast in bed sometime?"

"Yes, yes. But first I have to watch you do it."
He asked me how to work the coffee maker, and I
showed him. I think he already knew how to work
the toaster.

Then the morning after my birthday, after staying up very late, he crept out of bed while I was
sleeping. He had to make the coffee twice, because
the first time it didn't work — I don't know what he
did wrong. He poured the orange juice and made
the toast. Then he got the idea to add flowers. He
had to drive to the grocery store to get them, and
he was so worried that he'd wake me when starting
the car, ruining the surprise, that he pushed the car
out of the garage first. Then he brought me all
these things on a tray, and I was so, so surprised. I
made him take a picture of me with this breakfast.

Sergei's back had been seriously bothering him.
He'd done something to it just after the Olympics
while practicing a death spiral, then had hurt it
again while doing the Rodin number. Just before
my birthday, he had reinjured it in the gym. We
thought it was some sort of a slipped disc that was
pinching a nerve, because when it happened it sent
pain shooting all the way down to his toes. In fact,
he was losing the feeling in the toes of his left foot.

It was bothering him too much to practice. Still,
Marina came to Simsbury in late May so we could
begin working on our new program. She'd selected music from Grieg's Concerto in A minor with
orchestra, and the theme was that I was a weak
person, and Sergei must lift me up and get me

going. If I lose my energy and lie on the ice, Sergei will give me second life and give me power.

Marina always saw music in terms of either color or weather or seasons. This Grieg music she saw in waves, first very high, then very low. The high waves would be for the lifts. Then when the music fell low I would go around Sergei and lie down on the ice. Sergei would lay his hand on me and ask me to stand up. Marina would tell him, "You have the perfect warm hand; your hand should give her life." The music was almost like broken glass, much colder than the Rachmaninoff music that accompanied the Rodin program.

Sergei began seeing a wide array of doctors about his back. In Moscow, one doctor told him it was probably caused by air-conditioning from driving in the car. So we stopped using the air-conditioning. Still, his back continued to get worse. Sergei had problems even getting his foot into his skate boot because he couldn't straighten his toes. He couldn't skate. He took one step onto the ice, and he didn't feel his foot at all.

We went to see Dr. Abrams in Princeton. He had fixed the rotator cuff injury in Sergei's shoulder. After a series of tests confirmed that one of Sergei's discs in his back was quite swollen, Dr. Abrams told us it was a serious problem that might require surgery. We didn't like that idea at all.

We talked to Galina Zmievskaya, who knew a chiropractor in Odessa, in Ukraine, who had fixed a similar problem with Viktor Petrenko's back. She made us an appointment, and we flew immediately to Moscow. I stayed with my parents and Daria at our dacha, while Sergei bought a ticket to fly to Odessa to see Viktor's chiropractor. They sold him the ticket, no problem, but when he went to the plane, they told Sergei they had no more seats. But if you'd like to stand? So he stood the whole flight to Odessa in the place where the stewardesses work. Unbelievable.

The next day he went to the chiropractor, and this man began working on his back, rearranging things in the most agonizing fashion. Sergei couldn't even walk the next day. The doctor told him not even to try, just to lie down all day. "It's almost mini-surgery I did for you," the man said.

He worked on him one more time, two days later, then we flew back to the States. We started skating slowly—one day on, one day off. But Sergei still couldn't feel his foot on the ice. So we went to see Dr. Abrams again in Princeton, and he told us now that surgery might not be necessary. First he wanted to do more tests, one of which involved taking fluid out of Sergei's spine with a long needle. It made me crazy to even think about it. I was trying to talk to Sergei, to make him feel calm about the procedure, when I almost passed out. Sergei took one look at me and said, "Katia, what's going on with you?"

I felt like I had to sit or I'd faint. I didn't watch as they took the fluid out, but afterward Sergei felt so terrible they made him lie down for two hours before we could drive home. Sergei was never rude to me, ever. But this time I tried to ask him how he felt, and he was so mad about his back, so frustrated with the doctors and uncomfortable with the pain, that he didn't talk to me. I was almost afraid to ask him anything. He was reading his book and wouldn't even look at me.

Nothing helped the whole summer. The nerve in his left foot was so pinched that it was almost dead, so Dr. Abrams said he had to do physiotherapy for his foot. Sergei couldn't even stand on one leg. He couldn't stand on his tiptoes. He couldn't walk on his heels.

So every day he went to the gym and ran through a series of exercises. From mid-July to mid-August we were in Simsbury by ourselves, without Mom or Daria, but we were so frustrated we couldn't enjoy our time alone. We didn't take any romantic weekends or explore parts of New England we'd never seen. We were just trying to get Sergei healthy again.

All day long he exercised, for his back, for his stomach, for his foot. Four times a day he did special exercises for his foot. He worked too hard, if anything. I'd always been a little worried about Sergei, that maybe he wouldn't take his conditioning as seriously as he should when we were older. That he wouldn't care so much. I don't know. I can't explain, but I worried. But he showed me this summer that to take care of me and Daria, he would do anything. It was too much, some days.

He told me he felt terrible because he was not skating. He couldn't lift me, but he had to lift something. So all the time he was lifting weights. He couldn't run, because he couldn't feel his foot very well. So every other day we went to the swimming pool, and Sergei would swim fifty laps. He was working out almost twenty-four hours a day.

And day by day he got a little better, but slowly, so slowly. We decided to try to get ready for a pro-am competition being held in New Jersey in August. We started doing some lifts, and things were going fine. Daria and Mom had joined us in Simsbury, and every afternoon Sergei took Daria for a walk and played with her outside. He was such a good father. He'd become so strong, not only with his muscles, but as a person. More of a father. More of a husband. I felt so proud of him that summer.

Then one morning we started to do a spin together, and Sergei made a terrible scream. He tipped over, knocking me over as he fell.

"That's it," he said, lying there. It was the back again.

We called Jay and told him we couldn't do the pro-am competition, and we started to look for another doctor. The owner of the rink flew a doctor in from Florida who was a friend of his, and this man said Sergei had to do lots of exercises for his foot, and that he should have a lift put in the heel of his skate. But Sergei couldn't fit his foot in the skate when the lift was in, so it didn't do any good. Then a doctor from Simsbury took X rays of his back and started telling us all these terrible things about how badly his spine was shaped, how one leg was shorter than the other. I couldn't listen anymore. I didn't even want to translate the doctor's words for Sergei. It kept getting worse and worse.

In September we were supposed to go to Sun Valley to film *Pocahontas* for a television special. We'd worked with the Disney people before. In the past two years we'd also done television versions of *Cinderella* and *Aladdin*. It was good money and not very hard work. But Sergei still couldn't stand on his foot normally. Actually, we were in pretty terrible shape, because I couldn't fit my foot in my boot either because of a problem with corns. My left foot was useless, and Sergei's left foot was useless, so when we were skating it was just two feet for two skaters. Plus I'd lost about five pounds. I didn't eat anything, trying to be as light as possible for the times when Sergei had to lift me. I didn't know how else I could help him. We talked to the Disney people and told them that we couldn't really skate. But they said, It's okay, we're going to shoot you mostly off the ice. It's just a story. Sergei doesn't have to skate much. So we decided to go—all of us, including Mom and Daria, because Daria was going to have her third birthday.

It was quite a tight schedule. They had us skating on something about the size of an ice cube that was set in the middle of a forest, with leaves all over the ice. But they cleaned it all up. We only had one day to shoot the whole scene of Pocahontas—skating, on a horse, and in a canoe. All in six hours. I had recently cut my hair, and they were very surprised, because Pocahontas has long hair. They had to go get me some braids. Now I'm normal Pocahontas.

Relaxing in the hot springs at Sun Valley.

It was fun, but a lot of work. Not work, but standing around, waiting, many takes, too many to be standing in skates all the time with sore feet. The sun was right in our eyes, and I got sunburn. All the time they were rushing, rushing, because we had to do all these things before the sun went down. Finally they said they didn't have enough time to do both the canoe scene and the horse scene. They asked me which I would prefer.

I said I didn't know. "I'm not very good with horses, and I'm definitely terrible with canoes," I explained. "Whatever you wish." So they decided to try the horse scene. I talked to Sergei, and said, "Serioque, you know I'm afraid of horses. This one is going to bite me." A long time ago, a dog had bitten me twice, and since then I was sure that anything big like a horse would bite me. This was a very big horse. I had to come out of my tepee and lead this big horse—a young horse, not an old one—which was scary for me. I'm not good with animals. But this horse was good, and she waited for me calmly and listened to me, and Sergei was probably proud of me.

The best thing that came out of that trip was that Sergei met a trainer in Sun Valley who taught him he had to really warm up his muscles before he skated. So he stopped going to doctors and started seeing trainers. In Simsbury we saw another trainer who lay Sergei on a table, took him by the arms, then stretched him for forty-five minutes. Sergei felt better right away. He even felt taller. And that was the first time he smiled and believed that something was really helping him. This trainer also showed us a machine for the back, from which you hung upside down and did special exercises. This, too, seemed to help. We asked IMG if they would buy it for us so we could use it the whole season and take it with us on the tour. As it worked out, the manufacturer donated the machine and we had it sent to Lake Placid.

We had decided to forget competitions for a while and just focus on being able to skate the fifty-five-city tour. We again rented a condominium in Lake Placid so that Daria and my parents could visit us, but since Daria was already in school, they were just coming up on the weekends during the month of rehearsals. Everyone knew that Sergei had a problem with his back, and that we wouldn't be trying any difficult elements. We talked at length with Sandra Bezic and Michael Seibert, who were choreographing the group numbers. We were just going to take it easy for a while.

The television exhibition, Skates of Gold III, was also on our agenda. It was being held in Albany, and only Olympic gold medalists were invited. Since we were the only pairs skaters who could make it, they were very anxious that we come, and Sergei and I decided to skate to Verdi's *Requiem,* a program that Marina had made for us the year before. It was the easiest program we had in terms of technical difficulty.

We shared a limousine with Scott Hamilton and Kristi Yamaguchi, two other gold medalists in Stars on Ice. I told Sergei that when we skated in this Skates of Gold, not to express himself too much. To be careful with the lifts. No emotions, skate carefully, and everything will be fine. We had taken out the double axel. But we were both very nervous. I could see it in Sergei's face. We had to pay attention to every movement, and when we finished and everything had gone okay, it was such a great relief. The back had held up fine.

Sergei, though, was absolutely white. I didn't

know why, but he told me that on his very first
move, his lace had broken, and the longer the program went on, the looser it got. He didn't know
whether to stop or not. But after we did our last

Before the last Skates of Gold performance
(left to right) *Jenni Meno, an acquaintance, me, Sergei,*
Renee Roca, Brian Boitano, and Jayne Torvill.

jump, he decided he was going to stick it out
unless the skate actually fell off.

On the way back to Lake Placid with Scott and
Kristi, we had the limo stop at Wendy's. We'd
done exactly the same thing the year before after
Skates of Gold II. Sandwiches, salads, and french
fries, and then we talked the rest of the way back.
That stop was now our tradition. We decided we
would make this stop every year.

Goodbye

$\mathcal{M}$arina was coming to Lake Placid on Sunday, November 19, to help us work out the finishing touches of the Grieg program.

On Friday, Sergei and I skated a little bit in the afternoon session then went to see the movie *Goldeneye*, which Sergei liked very much. When we got back to the car, we noticed that the driver's-side rearview mirror was broken. We thought probably some young boy had done it. It was only later that I remembered that this was a sign of bad luck.

We went home, drank some Irish coffee, and spent a quiet, romantic evening in front of the fireplace, since it was a very cold night. Daria and my parents had stayed in Simsbury for the weekend. I don't remember why.

On Saturday we did nothing—our favorite kind of day. We woke late, went for a walk, and bought a lot of Christmas presents for Daria. Sergei bought her a skirt and a T-shirt, and together we picked out some hand-crafted decorations for our condominium. It was fun, shopping and walking through town.

On Sunday, since Marina wasn't due in until the afternoon, we again woke late, had a long breakfast, then just sat around. We didn't even go outside until we left for rehearsal at three o'clock. We had to rehearse the group numbers, choreographed by Sandra Bezic and Michael Seibert, with the entire cast. I have always been amazed how professional Sandra is in these situations. How confident she is. How she is able to control everyone so easily. She is a very beautiful, sexy woman, but also strong and powerful and creative. Everyone loves her.

At five o'clock Marina arrived. There are two rinks at the Lake Placid training center, and Sandra let Sergei and me leave the group rehearsal so we could work with Marina on the Grieg program at the smaller rink. We ran through everything, and, as often happened, if I wasn't doing something exactly the way Marina wanted it, she had me follow Sergei, to watch the way he moved his arms to the music. She added a double flip jump. One of the things we still needed to do was find an ending pose to the program, and that evening we found a beautiful one, in which Sergei laid me across his knee and touched my upturned face with his cupped hands, as if to say,

"Now, dear one, now you can rest." Marina said it would even be nice if I closed my eyes as if I were sleeping. We were satisfied that we were ready to perform this program for an audience.

We didn't leave the rink until nine-thirty at night. We had a reservation at a good restaurant, and by the time we got there, we were the only patrons. We had a nice, late dinner. Marina was in a good mood, the fireplace was blazing, and it was very, very cozy and comfortable. Marina talked a lot about some new programs she was thinking of doing for us, since there were now so many competitions every year—seven or even eight. She talked about her son, Fedor, who was thirteen, and we told her about Daria. We talked about costumes, Skate Canada, Skate America, Michelle Kwan—lots of fun skating talk. We left after midnight, I think.

The next morning we came over to the rink about ten o'clock. Marina had to leave that afternoon, before two, and we still had to rehearse the group number. The first hour we rehearsed with the others. I remember Marina was talking to designer Jef Billings about Sergei's costume. She said, "He's got big, beautiful arms, and he knows how to make beautiful movements with his arms, so you should not make a costume that covers his arms." Marina was worried that we wouldn't have enough time to work with her before her plane, since the group rehearsal was lasting so long. I was worried, too. But Sergei, who was always so calm, told us, "There'll be time. Don't worry."

Finally Sandra said that we could go. And Sergei, Marina, and I went to this smaller rink. We warmed up a little bit. We were both very happy with the changes she'd made in the program the night before, and decided we should skate through the whole number. Then Marina would have to go.

So we started. At the beginning I'm on one knee, and Sergei is on one knee, and we are face to face. I put my head on his shoulder, and I remember that his T-shirt smelled very clean. So I said, "Hmm, smells good."

And he said, "Yes, it's clean." Just this. These were the last words. Then we started to skate.

We did the early movements—the camel spin into a lift. The music goes low, and I circle around him and lie on the ice as if I'm getting tired. Sergei tries to help me get up. Then we do the big lift across the ice. He puts me down, and we do a side-by-side double flip, the new element Marina had added. We have good speed, and he throws me, a double axel throw, which I landed cleanly. He has to hurry to catch up with me. Then we were supposed to do two crossovers before another lift.

The full orchestra was just coming in, one of those high waves of music Marina liked so much. Sergei was gliding on the ice, but he didn't do the crossovers. His hands didn't go around my waist for the lift. I thought it was his back. He was bent over slightly, and I asked him, "Is it your back?" He shook his head a little. He couldn't control himself. He tried to stop, but he kept gliding into the boards. He tried to hold onto the boards. He was dizzy, but Sergei didn't tell me what was happening. Then he bent his knees and lay down on the ice very carefully. I kept asking what was happening. "What's wrong, Serioque? What's the matter?" But he didn't tell me. He didn't speak at all.

Marina stopped the music. When she came over to him, she knew right away it was something with his heart. It looked like he couldn't breathe anymore. She told me to call 911, and Marina started doing CPR on him. I was so scared. I was screaming, I don't know what. I forgot all the words in English. I couldn't remember the word for help. I ran to the other rink, crying, to get someone to call 911 for me.

By the time I got back, everyone was around him, and the medical people were working on him, trying to get his heart going. He didn't have normal color in his face. It was turning blue, and some white stuff was coming from his mouth. They wouldn't let me get close to him. The other skaters were holding me. They didn't want to let me watch what was happening. Then they were taking him in the ambulance, and I only had time to get my skates off and pick up Sergei's bag. I sat in the front because they didn't want me to see as they worked on him in the back.

I looked at the clock when we got to the hospital, and it was 11:35. I saw on the monitor that was attached to him that Sergei's heart was still beating. It was a wavy line, not a straight line. I was very worried, but I didn't think it could be something so terrible. I really thought he would be fine. I never even let myself think for a minute he might die. The doctors asked us some questions about Sergei's history, whether he'd ever had any heart problems before. We told them no. We told them if he needed an operation, to do it right away. Don't wait to ask. Don't waste a moment. Marina and I walked around the hospital while we waited, and she talked to me all the time.

Then a woman doctor came out to talk to us. Her face was very serious. She said they had given the electric shocks. She said they had given him the shot of Adrenalin in the heart. But they had lost Sergei.

When I translated these words in my head, it was very difficult to understand. I didn't want to understand. My heart was scared, but I understood all right. And the first thing that came into my head was, How would I tell Mom? How would I tell Daria? How would I tell Sergei's mom? When I started to say these concerns to Marina, she told me to put this out of my mind. "Go talk to Sergei," she said. "He can still hear you."

The doctors didn't want to let me go see him alone. I suppose they were afraid I would do something crazy. They still had to do the autopsy.

But Marina told them it would be okay. They told me that Sergei still had two tubes in his mouth, and that these tubes had to stay in there, and not to be scared of them.

I can't describe the feelings that went through me when I walked into the room where Sergei was lying, his skates still on his feet. He didn't look dead. It looked like he was just sleeping. Even one eye was open a little bit, and the whole time I thought that maybe he was looking at me. He even looked like he was breathing. His hands were cold, but when I felt his shoulders and chest, they were still warm.

It was very difficult for me to start talking to him. I didn't know what to say. I don't even remember what I began talking about. It was very simple. Something like, "Your hands are so cold." I apologized, too. "Sorry, Serioque. I'm so sorry." Once I got started, I got used to speaking to him, got used to the tubes in his mouth, and was able to say things to him normally. As I talked, I was thinking, He will never stand up. He will never take me in his arms again, never hug me again, never hold my hand again. But it will be a long time before I believe it.

I was in there a long time. Marina also came in and held his hand and talked to Sergei. I tried not to listen. Then I started to take off his skates, and his feet were very cold. I tried to warm them up by rubbing them. I rubbed them and rubbed them. I tried to warm his hands up, too. I loved his hands very much, loved the way they were so big and soft. But I couldn't make them warm.

It's not clear in my memory how the rest of the day unfolded. It seemed to go on forever. Marina stayed with me the whole time, every second. We realized we had to make some calls, and I called my mom first. She and Dad were going to fly up with Debbie Nast and Viktor Petrenko in a plane that Debbie had chartered. Daria was staying in Simsbury with Viktor's wife, Nina.

Back at the condominium, Marina started asking me lots of questions about Sergei. What kind of food does he like? What kind of flowers? I told her he liked tulips, and she had a book with her about the significance of all the flowers, and looked it up. Tulips were the flower of luck. Then we looked up his symbol on the zodiac, which was Aquarius. This sign, we learned, stood for wisdom, and arms, and wings, and the flight of birds, and youth. The motto of Aquarius is, Don't sacrifice love for your friendships. He didn't. Sergei had lots of very close friendships, but his love for me always came first.

Then Christine "Tuffy" Hough, Scott, and Kristi came to see me, to see if it was all right for all the skaters to come visit. Of course, I said. Everyone loved Sergei so much. They were all crying. We looked at the lake and talked about how unbelievable it was, and cried. Sergei was so big, and strong, and solid. Now he was gone.

Sometimes, if I let my mind forget a little while,

just go blank and think of nothing, it seemed like Sergei was just out of the room, and that he would come back in a minute to see all his friends. I was so used to him being around me. I kept half expecting him to come through the door. Or that I could reach him by phone if I had to.

I was not used to sleeping by myself. That first night, when I awoke and felt cold in my bed, a knifeblade of fear went through me as I realized I hadn't been dreaming. Please, God, why couldn't I have been dreaming? It would all come back, flooding my memory like ice crystals on a river, and I would quietly shiver, the hot tears burning my eyes. In the months that followed, sleep became my ally. I longed to sleep all the time, to sleep without waking, to dream without living.

There was never any question where the burial would be. Sergei had a Russian soul. He was only comfortable there. But before we returned to Moscow, Debbie Nast arranged for a wake at the funeral home in Saranac Lake, to give the other skaters a chance to say goodbye. The man at the funeral home had asked me to bring some clothes for Sergei. He didn't say to bring a jacket and tie and shoes and socks and everything. So I only brought the black pants he'd recently bought, before the Skates of Gold, and a black cashmere sweater. He looked wonderful in this outfit. He had told me he liked it very much.

At this wake, I went in first to say goodbye. It was a small room, filled with flowers. Sergei looked like he was sleeping. He had an expression on his face almost like he wanted to smile. Very peaceful and handsome. The man at the funeral home had given me Sergei's wedding ring, which I put on a chain to wear around my neck. He had told me I could put anything I wanted in the casket with Sergei—a letter, even, if I wanted to write one. I did write a letter to him. But I couldn't put it in with him, because everything I wished to say, as soon as I wrote it down, seemed slightly wrong, slightly different from what I had intended. So instead I tucked a picture of Daria in the front of his pants. New York to Moscow was a long way to go, and I thought the trip would be better if he had a keepsake of Daria with him.

Then my parents went in. Then Viktor. I brought Scott in myself. He had always tried very hard to get Sergei to laugh, and Sergei felt comfortable with him. We knelt by the open coffin, and I showed him the picture I had left with Sergei of Daria. I whispered to Scott, "It was too perfect, maybe. It's only fairy tales that have happy endings. Everything was too good with me and Sergei for it to end happily."

He squeezed my hand. Then the others came in, too, everyone getting a chance to say a proper goodbye. They all held my hand, and Paul Wylie, who is very religious, said some words to God about protecting Sergei's soul and watching over Daria and me. There was a book for everyone to sign. The whole experience gave me comfort, and

I was happy that my close friends were with me. Sergei was still so beautiful, even in death. In my mind, that will always be the last day I had with my Seriozha.

That night, very late, we drove back to Simsbury to pack for the trip to Moscow. Daria, of course, would come, too, and there was the question of what to say to her. How to tell her. Whether to say anything at all. My mother thought at first we should tell her that her father was away training. She was certainly used to us being away. But then Daria's teacher from nursery school called to find out how long she would be gone.

I asked her what she thought I should tell Daria. She didn't know, but she said she would talk to the school psychologist and call me right back. When she did, she told me that it was important that I explain what had happened before someone else tried. She said not to be afraid to use the words "He's dead and will never come back." She told me to explain that everyone will be very upset with this, and a lot of people will be crying. She said, don't expect Daria to cry and scream, or even, necessarily, be upset. She cannot understand the word *death* and all it implies. But it's important that she hear it from her mother.

The next morning, I did this. I didn't tell my mother what I was planning. I just sat Daria down and we talked. It was very, very difficult to start, difficult even for me to say the words: "Your father is dead; he's not coming back." And, as the teacher had said, Daria didn't cry or get upset. But she asked, "How can we see him?" So I told her that her father would come see her whenever he wants, and that sometimes she'd see him in her dreams. That he was like a little angel now. But that he'd never come back to her as we knew him, and that it was very sad, and sometimes I would be crying, and that would be the reason. I looked carefully into her eyes as I spoke these words, so she'd understand. And I think she did understand, at least as far as it was possible. Because when we were back in Moscow, Daria wore a cross around her neck on a chain. And a few times she held this cross up to people and said, her face very sad, "You know, God took my father."

In Moscow, it was all so different, everything rushed, everything crowded, everything crazy. The first day I arrived I went to see Sergei's mother, Anna, who was mad with grief. Her apartment was filled with relatives, men and women I had never met before, most of whom had not seen Sergei since he was a little boy. Everyone wanted to show their emotions and their tears. No one was holding anything back, which was so different from Sergei, who believed in not showing his pain. First one would cry, then another would cry, then another and another. They fed off each other's misery. All the time, they were crying. I felt so badly for Sergei's sister, Natalia, and her daughter, Svetlana, who had to stay there with all these crying relatives.

There was one lady, perhaps an aunt, who was reading the Bible all the time in front of Sergei's picture. Everyone wanted to say something to me, what they thought about this tragedy, but not necessa...rily something nice. Even though they had seen Sergei maybe twice in their life, they thought of Sergei as theirs, and now they had lost him, and they would talk to me about their loss.

Even Anna was taking it so differently from me. It's not possible to compare my loss with her loss, but when she talked to me about him, it was always about how she remembered him as a very little boy. All her memories of him were of when he was small. This Sergei, the one she missed so, had long ago passed from the world. We had traveled so much, had seen so little of our parents. Anna had never been out of the country before. She had never seen the kind of life that we had made for ourselves. She blamed skating for his heart attack. That Sergei's dear father had had four heart attacks did not factor into her thinking. She told me I didn't take good enough care of her son. All these things that I could not bear to hear.

It was cold and bleak the day of the funeral. The service was held at the ice rink of the Central Red Army Club, which had twelve thousand seats, most of them filled with mourners, with thousands more filing past Sergei's casket, which lay open at center ice. Before the service, some of Sergei's relatives were asking me why he was not in a jacket. Why he wasn't wearing a tie. They drove me crazy with this talk about clothes. When they found out about the picture of Daria I'd put in his pants, they thought I'd gone mad. They told me, It's not supposed to be this way.

Then, just before the service was to begin, as Father Nikolai was singing for Sergei, one of the relatives said Sergei was lying in the wrong direction, that his head was supposed to be to the north. So they started to move the casket. I couldn't believe it. I asked them to please stop. Father Nikolai, fortunately, intervened. He was performing the service, and he told them the casket was okay where it was, that it was fine.

All the skaters from the Russian All-Stars were there, as well as Tatiana Tarasova, Viktor, Paul Wylie, Scott, Zaharov. Leonovich flew in from France; Artur Dmitriev came from Saint Petersburg; Jay and Debbie from IMG; Bob Young from the International Skating Center. And Marina, of course. Plus so many others I don't remember. It was so great to see them. It meant so much that his friends had come to tell him goodbye. The Central Red Army Club had arranged for Sergei to be buried in Vagankovskoy Cemetery, which was a very great honor; it was the place where many famous Russians were laid to rest. And when we drove from the service to this cemetery, people were waiting along the route to see us pass, and some of them were even sitting in the trees.

Zhuk was there, too. I couldn't believe it. He'd been drinking, and he talked to me afterward at the reception. He hadn't changed. He started talking to me about this lady who had given me the magic metal disc to cover my weak hole. Remember? The spot beneath my left shoulder blade. Zhuk said that this lady knew that this tragedy was going to happen to Sergei. He said, "You have to go to her and apologize for the time that you and Sergei lost contact with her. You have the same problem as he did, and you'd better go talk to her now." I couldn't believe what I was hearing.

He wasn't the only one to say things that hurt me, however. Sergei's mother said some things, too. But it's okay, because I know that she was in pain, and that I, too, probably said things that hurt people during this awful time. I told my mother later, we were crazy in those days, absolutely crazy with grief. We were dreaming terrible dreams, thinking terrible thoughts. The autopsy had showed that Sergei, in addition to having blocked arteries near his heart, had also suffered a mild, undetected heart attack the day before he died. How could I not have known this? How could I not have suspected that his back problems—the spasms, the numbness in his foot—were warning signs of something much worse? I wrote in my diary that I didn't deserve Sergei, that I was glad to be hurt so deeply by God, because I didn't have time to give Sergei the love he should have been given. I was very hard on myself.

Sometimes I was angry at God, too. Or angry

at life. But most often I was angry at myself. It was easier for me to think I didn't deserve to have this happiness longer, that it was somehow my mistake, that I did something wrong, than to think that God was so ungenerous as to take Sergei away.

In those first few weeks, I went often to visit Father Nikolai. He said not to think this way, not to believe that Sergei's death was my mistake, or the result of anything I did to make God angry. He comforted me by telling me that I would meet Sergei again. He said he knew it was difficult to believe this, but I do believe it. I remember what Sergei told his sister, Natalia, after her boyfriend, Dmitri, had died. I think that Sergei's soul now lives somewhere. In our religion, we have two very important days after a death: the ninth day and the fortieth day. From the day of the death until the ninth day, the deceased is still with us, and people will dream about him very clearly. Then on the ninth day the deceased starts his journey to the gates that open either to Paradise or to Hell. God will decide where He wants this person. On the fortieth day, he leaves us. He's free. He now has his own spiritual life.

Losing Myself

I spent one night alone in the studio apartment where Sergei and I had begun our married life. We had almost no furniture there, just a bed and a television on the floor. But I loved this place with all my heart. I felt close to Sergei's spirit there. So many memories. So many special times that just the two of us shared. But after this one night, I couldn't go there anymore. I just couldn't. I said goodbye to this sweet place. I knew I should be staying with Daria.

I was living with my parents, taking life one day at a time. Marina had left a whole list of things I should do—go to the ballet, to an art gallery, to the circus, to the symphony. I'd never sat through an entire symphony before. I did all these things. But only half of my mind was there. Probably less than half.

I felt I was slowly losing myself. My strength was ebbing away. I had no purpose in my life, nothing to strive for. My parents were there to take care of Daria, so I didn't have that to worry about. All I was doing was dealing with my feelings, and this was killing me. When I opened my eyes in the morning, I'd lie in bed wondering, Why do I awaken? What do I have to get out of bed for? I had no pressing responsibilities. Nothing to train for. No future I cared to think about. No Sergei. Always the thoughts ended there. No Seriozha to lead me out of this unending darkness.

My mother told me that if I didn't want to skate ever again, that I could stop right then. That I could stay with her, and she would support me. She had enough money for the next ten years. Jay had told me not to worry about my finances, that things would be fine. They were trying to put together a benefit. Debbie called me every other day and said that people were sending in donations to Sergei's memorial fund. The response from people we had touched through our skating had been overwhelming. I never thought the whole world would think about Daria and me. So it was not money that concerned me. It was my broken heart. My mother said, Daria doesn't need a sick mom. She needs a healthy mom. Whether you live in Moscow or go back to America, try to come back as a healthy person.

It was then that I began to realize that work is the only thing that can help people heal. At least, it was what could help me heal. I still had skating. I was always a skater first, and to lose both Sergei and skating was more than I could handle. Ever since I was four years old, every day I either put on my skates or I worked on something that was related to my skating. Now I needed this focus in my life again. So I called Viktor, who had returned to Simsbury, and asked him to send me my skates. No problem, he said. To Viktor, favors were always no problem. He had taken Sergei's death very, very deeply, and I could feel he, too, was in pain.

The skates arrived in mid-December. In the mornings, I started practicing at the Central Red Army Club rink, so now at least I had a reason to get out of bed. It felt good to be again touching the ice that was so dear to Sergei and me. All those memories I had of being on the ice with Sergei, I could hold onto them there very gently. I had no inkling of what might become of it, but it was good for me to see the coaches and young skaters working on their elements, smiling. Life was going on. This was the first step.

Marina called me every few days. She had been having almost as hard a time as I had. She'd been sending letters to me in Moscow, letters of terrible sadness, some of which had made me so upset I couldn't finish them in one sitting. She had written to me that Sergei had been her dream, and now this dream had died. She was feeling much older now. She couldn't work and didn't know what to live for anymore. She thought, in her grief, these words were okay for my ears and my eyes.

On the phone, however, she wasn't like this. In one of our conversations I told Marina that the tribute to Sergei's memory had been arranged, a skating exhibition by all of our dear friends celebrating his life. They wanted me to walk out onto the ice and maybe say something. But this was unthinkable to her. Marina said if they were going to do the show, I should skate in it. She would create a program for me.

It was difficult for me to imagine myself skating in front of people without holding Sergei's hand, without looking into Sergei's eyes, looking only at the audience, trying to fill that huge ice surface all by myself. But if I were to skate in the exhibition, that was how it would have to be. I wasn't going to skate with another partner. It was inconceivable to think of someone else's arms around me on the ice, touching me. Sergei's was the only hand I had held on the ice since I was eleven years old.

I talked to Father Nikolai about this idea, to see if it would be all right for me to skate, appropriate for a period of mourning, which in the Russian church lasts for one year. Father Nikolai, who was always so gentle, said, "Katia, please skate, because I know you love to do it, and your skating brings happiness to others." Then he added,

"Don't worry about being happy in your future life. Sergei will even help you with this. When you find someone else, bring him back to this church, no matter what his religion or nationality. I will bless this union, and that will be Sergei's blessing, too."

These words brought me comfort, as Father Nikolai's words always did. But the kindness of this man could not shield me from a side of life I'd soon see, frightening and abhorrent, that I'd been spared when I was living with Sergei. One day Zaharov, our former coach, called me and said that a businessman he knew wanted to talk to me. He said this man sponsored boxers and wrestlers, and he might be a big help in my future career.

I met this man in Zaharov's room. We talked a little bit, and the man said he also supported children's funds, and that he would like to give some of this money to Daria. He handed me an envelope for her. Later, when I opened it, I was shocked to find how much money was inside. I didn't know what to do. I called him back to say thanks, that it was very generous of his fund to think of Daria.

He called me a couple more times, then invited me to a big dinner. He told me he had relatives in Paris, money in France, money in America, money in Germany. We have so many people like this in Russia now. I don't know where they get all this money.

So I went to this dinner, and I thought he was going to tell me about some marketing idea. I was so naive. I don't know what I was thinking. He told me he had followed Sergei's and my career for a long time, and said he wanted to give me a car. He asked what kind of car I'd like to have. I thought it was all a joke, and said, "I like Jaguars. Are you going to give me a Jaguar?" He said, "Okay, I'll ask around." Then he called another time and said, "I've found a Jaguar. You want me to buy it for you?" Only now was it clear to me. I said, "No, I don't want you to buy me a Jaguar, thank you." He said, "You need an apartment. I'm going to buy you an apartment." So he's probably right now off looking for an apartment for me, thinking I'm going to live there.

I felt terrible. I tried to give him this money back that he'd given to Daria, but he said, "No, this is not for you, it's for her. You must keep it." And this man wasn't the only one to frighten me. There were others, too. I became very, very upset with Russian life. Everything was so different for me now. With Sergei, I knew I was safe. Sergei would pick up the phone when it rang, and if I didn't want to talk to the person who called, I didn't have to. Now just anyone could call me and say they could help me, say they would like to meet me, say they will make me happier. This is not what these people wanted, to make me happier.

When I told my mom about these things, she said, "You're going to have to learn a lot of things that you never learned before, about life and about people. You're just too honest with people. You think they always wish you the best. But absolutely not. They do not always wish you the best."

So I made an important decision. When I returned to Moscow, I didn't know what I'd do with my future. I didn't know if I would try to continue to skate. I didn't know if I was going to come back to the United States. I just didn't know. But after a couple of these terrible situations, I definitely decided that I had to go back to the United States. I had to go back to Simsbury, where Sergei and I had started to make a home for ourselves. I was losing myself totally. Life in Russia had changed so much from the days when I was growing up.

First, however, I wanted to spend another New Year's with my parents and sister. That isn't exactly right. In hindsight, I'm so grateful I had this experience, but at the time I wasn't sure if I wanted to be with them or not. They were spending New Year's at their new dacha in Ligooshina. They had built it from logs to replace the old cabin in which Sergei, Moshka, and I had spent ten lovely days in 1989. My father had invited a lot of his friends, and because it was going to be mostly people my parents' age, I didn't know if I'd enjoy it or not. I thought I'd probably feel out of place, except that I loved the dacha, I loved the sauna, and New Year's was a family holiday. My mom kept asking me to go. And my sister, at the last minute, decided to be there. And, as it turned out, my parents' friends all brought their kids, who were the same age as my sister—no longer kids at all, but aged eighteen, nineteen, and twenty. It turned into quite a little party.

There were twelve of us in all, and this was the first time since Sergei's death that I laughed. Really laughed. One friend of my sister's whom I remember from when I was twelve years old began

Our sauna in the country,
my first New Year's without Sergei.

telling these jokes, and I was laughing so hard I could cry. Also a young boy named Maxime—not so young, twenty years old, only four years younger than me—was asking my opinion about whether to continue playing his sport, Olympic handball, or if he should turn to business in order to support his family. He was recently married and felt he had to begin earning more money. And it was also difficult because his father was his coach. It was the first time that anyone sought my advice about something so serious. "Maxime," I said. "Just continue. You are young only once."

We were drinking champagne, and we were swimming in snow, because there was so much snow on the ground that winter. Hills of it, almost like Lillehammer. The weather was beautiful, and at sunset the red sun painted the white snow a fiery pink with its rays. It was so lovely. But it was also very sad, because I didn't have my Seriozha around me. I was thinking, Why on such a great day, in such gorgeous weather, is he not here?

My father had cut two Christmas trees from the forest, one for inside the dacha and one for outside on the steps. We put all the gifts under the Christmas tree that was inside, and there were far too many this year for the Santa bag that my grandmother had sewn, because all our guests had brought their gifts, too.

And that night, for the first time since 1988, we remembered the tradition of breaking the plate at midnight and making a wish. Because there were twelve people, this time my mother dropped two plates. I was with Daria. We decided we would hide one piece together and make the wish. Because she was so small, I thought everyone would give us some room once the plates were broken, so her little hand could find a nice piece. But I was wrong. At the first stroke of midnight, my mother smashed the plates, and everyone was like—vrooom! It was like a bunch of little kids scrambling for candy. We were nearly trampled to death. Daria and I took the last broken piece of plate we could find and ran off to my parents' bedroom. We hid this piece under the wardrobe in the corner. I can't tell you what I wished, or it will never come true. But this wish I made for Daria.

After this wonderful New Year's night, I flew home to Simsbury as soon as I could pack and make the arrangements. Home, that's now what Connecticut seemed like to me. And I decided it would be terrible—impossible, in fact—for me to come home without Daria.

My parents were pretty upset by this, I think. Daria was the joy of their life now, and they were so used to having her with them. They weren't coming to Connecticut for another month, and they didn't want Daria to be there alone with me. They were still unsure about my frame of mind, whether I was strong enough to care for two people, instead of just one. But I didn't want to discuss it with them. I couldn't do it any other way. I don't know how I found the strength to say, "Mom, I'm going to take her. This is my decision." But I did. And I'll always be happy I did.

The Tribute

A few days after we'd returned to the States, Daria asked me about Sergei for the first time since his death. She had just woken up, and instead of getting right out of bed and going down to the playroom, as she usually did, she sat quietly by herself for a long while. Then she came into my bedroom and said, "Mom, I miss Father. I want to see him."

It was the first thing out of her mouth, so perhaps she'd had a dream about him. This was very, very hard for me. I held her in my lap and said, "Dasha, remember what I told you? About how Dad isn't coming back? How he died? Only when you sleep can you see him, maybe, if you really, really try." Then I put my face up close to hers and looked into her bright blue eyes, which were Sergei's eyes. "Can you see Father in my eyes?" I asked. She shook her head no. "I can see him in yours."

We went to Ottawa later in the month, so Marina could create the program for me to skate at Sergei's tribute, which was going to be held in Hartford on February 27. Marina had already chosen the music. It was Gustav Mahler's Symphony no. 5, *IV Adagietto*. I had always liked this music, which is sensitive and tender and also a little bit sad. Marina told me that Mahler wrote this music when he was proposing to his wife; that, in fact, the music served as his proposal; that he gave it to her, and she sat down at the piano and played it, and the music did his speaking for him. His wife immediately understood. Marina never thought a couple could skate to it, however. She saw this music only as a skating solo.

When we first listened to it on the ice, she said to me, "I don't know what to do." Then we listened more, and the music told us what to do. Marina said to me, "Imagine that you're skating with Sergei for the last time." Then, "Now you've lost him, you're missing him, you're looking for him and can't find him. You get on your knees and ask God why it happened. Your legs feel broken, as if they have no strength. You cannot move. Everything inside you feels broken, too. You must ask God for some help. You must tell God you understand that life goes on, and now you have to skate. You must thank Him for giving you Sergei for half of your life, the most beautiful time in your life. This is about how all people can get up from their knees in the face of adversity, can go forward, can have the strength to persevere. You can find someone to live for. You can have a life of your own now."

No one else in the world could have created this program for me. I was thinking afterward that Marina was a miracle that God had given to Sergei and me. He took Sergei, but he left me Marina. She understood Sergei to his soul, and sometimes I think that Marina knows me better than I know myself. Even if no one else understood this number, Sergei, Marina, and I would understand it. It was easier for me to think of Marina and me performing it for him together. She had been having a very hard time with her work, but for him she had summoned the strength to create this beautiful program.

It was very, very difficult for me to skate it, however. First it was strange to be skating alone, without Sergei's hand to hold me and take care of me. Something so simple as a layback spin is not an element we did in pairs, so it was the first time I'd done one since I was eleven years old, and it hurt my back. Most important, to skate this number emotionally every time is impossible. So it's difficult to practice it right. The first time I performed it before a small audience of friends and coaches in Ottawa, so we could get their reaction and see if I was strong enough to do it properly, I felt no power at all. I had to think about every movement—now I'm doing this, now I'm doing this—and afterward I was exhausted. I was never comfortable or relaxed. It became very clear to me that emotions can make your legs so weak you're unable to jump, and that I had to train harder if I was really going to perform.

After that little exhibition, I had to fly to New York to do an interview with CBS, since the network was airing the tribute. I left Daria with Marina, so I was traveling by myself. I couldn't remember traveling anywhere by myself before. Always it was with Sergei, or my mom, or Debbie, or Daria. I was shy and a little afraid. Only now was I beginning to understand what a trial it was to go through life alone. How unnatural it was. For solace I was keeping a journal, but the words that I wrote on the paper weren't the same words as I had in my head, because every moment my thoughts were different.

When I was back in Moscow, Marina had written to me that with Sergei's death, she said goodbye to her dream. I didn't understand what she meant at first. But perhaps with Marina, and others, their time with Sergei was like a dream. For me, however, this dream was my everyday life, normal and real. Only now did I understand I had to say goodbye to not only my dream, but my happiness, my normal life, which perhaps I didn't appreciate enough.

People had been telling me ever since he died that it's unbelievable what happened. But not to me. I believed it too much. I watched it happen. I saw it and felt it. When Sergei died, it was like he passed right through me. I understood it with every fiber in my being. From the very first words the doctor said when she told me that Sergei had died, I believed, not with my ears, but with my heart.

And I continued to wonder, Why would God give me this man in the first place, then take him away? Did He want to show me how difficult life is? How much the heart can hurt? I never thought I'd feel heartache like this. I'd read in books about heartache, and never understood it. I thought it was just words on paper that the poets wrote. But now I well understand this feeling. It's physical pain, sharp pangs that I got every time I remembered things I should have told Sergei, but didn't. Things I could have done to show him that I loved him, but didn't. In Russia, we have an expression: *Kamen na serdce.* Your heart feels like there's a rock on it, it's so heavy. And this described mine.

❖ ❖ ❖

In our religion, once the fortieth day has passed after the death of a loved one, it is no longer necessary to think of them all the time. More than that, it is no longer proper for you to do so, because it means that you're holding onto them. You have to release people. If God wants to take them away, then that is the road they must go down, and it is wrong for you to try to interfere.

I had a dream in early February, just before Sergei's birthday. He would have been twenty-nine. It was a very bad dream, very scary. Sergei was so mad at me in this dream. He was in a hospital, and we all knew that he was going to die. But it was very difficult for him to understand this. Someone was trying to explain it to him, maybe I was, and Sergei was shouting at me, very angry. He was showing me that something disturbed him. He was telling me he was in a difficult situation, and I wasn't making it any easier.

It frightened me terribly. I was so scared after waking up. I told my mom about this dream, because I didn't understand it. She didn't understand it either, but she told me that everything that happens brings some good with it. "There's something good in this dream," she said. "Maybe you'll find it."

The next day I felt much better for having told my mother about the dream, and I was smiling all day. It was February 4, Sergei's birthday, and it was like he didn't want me to be sad on his birthday. Before this dream, I'd blamed myself for his death, but afterward, it was like Sergei had told me, "This is what I wanted, so leave me. Release me."

I began thinking that it could have been worse. People look for comfort wherever they can find it, but who knows? No one knows what might have happened in a couple of years. Maybe this was the easier way. Sergei only lived through the best years. He never had to live through his worst ones. He never did anything bad to anyone. He never suffered, or caused suffering. So I don't know. Maybe it was all for the best.

The whole month leading up to his tribute night, I was extremely nervous. Not only was I skating by myself for the first time since I was eleven, but I had to play the role of the hostess. Jay and Debbie had asked me who I wanted to skate in the show, and I told them Marina Klimova and Sergei Ponomarenko, Alexander Fadeev, Viktor Petrenko, and Oksana Baiul. Maybe Yuka Sato would be nice, because Sergei had always admired her skating. I remember him watching her on television in the 1992 Olympics and being very excited. Brian Boitano said that if there's going to be a show, he'd like to skate in it. Marina's thirteen-year-old son, Fedor Andreev, to whom Sergei had always been like a brother, was included too. Plus the Stars on Ice cast—Scott and Kristi and Kurt and Rosalynn and the rest—who were like family to us. Others were asking if they could skate in the show, too—Brian Orser, Lloyd and Isabelle, Paul Martini and Barbara Underhill, Maia Usova and Alexander Zhulin, Artur Dmitriev and his new partner. But we were too limited with time to invite everyone.

Sergei's mom, Anna, also came. It was the first time she'd been out of Russia. Anna stayed with me and my parents in the condominium in Simsbury, and it meant a great deal to me to have her there. Of course it was difficult, too. My parents hadn't seen very much of her over the years, and now we all lived together under the same roof for a couple of very emotional weeks. Even in the best of circumstances, families have differences. It was tough. The only thing that particularly upset my parents was that Anna was always crying, and it made Daria cry. Anna saw the pictures of Sergei all over the walls, on the tables, in every room, and it made her cry. And dear Daria, with her little heart, came to her and asked, "Why are you crying, Grandmother? Why do you cry?"

And Anna responded, "Why do I cry? Child, because my son has died. Why do I have to tell this to you?"

She would carry on about how she was talking to Sergei in her dreams, how he had worked too hard in this sport. She said some things that were not easy to listen to. Anna was crazy with sadness. I don't blame her for these words. But it was hell, at times. It was hell.

When the other skaters arrived the day before the show, seeing all Sergei's dear friends made me very relieved and happy. I was particularly pleased that no one talked to me like a sick person, that they didn't keep asking me how I was. We had a press conference and a few interviews, then three or four hours to rehearse the two group numbers at the International Skating Center in Simsbury. Afterward I was hosting a dinner. Everyone was so professional. Sandra Bezic and Michael Seibert, who had created an opening procession to the *Moonlight* Sonata, were accustomed to working in a big group. But Marina wasn't. She'd never done a group number before. And it was Marina who choreographed the beautiful closing number, which was to the String Serenade from Tchaikovsky's Fifth Symphony. Its meaning expressed exactly what the show was about: the celebration of a life.

Marina had brought Polaroids of all the different poses that Sergei and I had done in our programs over the years. From the Rodin number. From *Romeo and Juliet*. From *Moonlight* Sonata. All romantic poses. The skaters paired up, and everyone assumed one of these poses, all of them taking it very seriously. I knew right then they would skate perfectly the next night.

Vladislav Kostin, our costume designer from the Bolshoi Theater, had come, and he created the white dress that I would wear in this finale. Tatiana Tarasova also was there. I was feeling so much better after seeing everyone, feeling that they'd come to support me, come to Hartford for Sergei, to do what they loved to do. And I knew that they'd wanted to come with all their heart. I can't describe what this meant to me, except to say I didn't even worry about the show anymore. The only thing I was worried about was the dinner beforehand, because I knew I couldn't invite everyone. My house was too small, and I didn't want anyone to be upset.

We rehearsed again the next day at the Hartford Civic Center, where the show was being held. Marina stressed everyone out, which was unusual. In the Lillehammer Olympics she was also nervous, but she'd kept herself composed. Here, she was nervous, but also weak. She couldn't decide on things, not even on which dress I should wear, which wasn't like her. She had been so sad since Sergei's death, like a flower that had so much energy, but now had lost its bloom. Marina did find the words, however, to give me strength before I skated that night. "Just trust Sergei," she said, "and he will help you."

I wasn't in the opening processional number. I was waiting behind the curtain, not watching for fear that I would cry and lose my composure. When I heard the music of *Moonlight* Sonata, so many memories came back. I found myself going through my movements for our free program from the 1994 Olympics. Here Sergei throws me. Here we spin. Here we cross over. Here we do the side-by-side jump. I couldn't stop myself. I didn't want to stop myself. I felt Sergei's spirit was beside me right then.

As the time neared for my solo number, I thought about the words Sergei used to say to me when we were getting ready to skate. We always kissed each other before we skated, we always hugged and touched each other. Now, in the tunnel, waiting to go on the ice, I didn't have anyone to touch or kiss. It was a terrible feeling to be standing there by myself. Only Dave, the production manager for Stars on Ice, was there watching, and I could tell he was thinking the same thing: How sad to see her standing here without Sergei.

Then I thought of what Marina had said: Just trust Sergei, and he will help you. It felt like there was a rock in my throat, and I knew if I started to get emotional, I'd never be able to stop.

But as soon as the Mahler music started to play, and I skated out into the darkened arena, the bad feelings went away. The lights rose, the people started to applaud, and I had a feeling I'd never experienced before. I'd been worried that I'd be lost out there by myself, that I'd be so small no one would see me. But I felt so much bigger than I am. I felt huge, suddenly, like I filled the entire ice.

As the people clapped at the beginning of the program, I wondered whether I should stop. I wanted to thank them for coming from all over the country, all over the world, to think of Sergei. But my legs kept moving. I thought, I can't stop or I'll lose all this magic and power. I just listened to my legs. And I listened to Sergei. It was like I had double power. I never felt so much power in myself, so much energy. I'd start a movement, and someone would finish it for me. I didn't have a thing in my head. It was all in my heart, all in my soul.

I'll never be able to skate this number as well again. I don't want to skate it again. It was such a special thing, and I don't know if Sergei would help me a second time.

When I had finished, I couldn't control my emotions. I saw Daria. I saw Sergei's mother. I saw the people standing and clapping. I was happy, but I had tears in my chest, and they wanted to fall out. I didn't want to cry, because it was supposed to be a celebrational evening, commemorating the happy years Sergei and I had together. But some things you cannot control. And the other skaters were all standing and crying. They were all so proud of me. I wanted to hug every one of them. And I wanted to hug Marina, who was standing at the edge of the ice so I would remember which way to exit. She said she was going to wait until I saw her, and then leave. But she couldn't leave.

I remember that Marina still looked very, very sad at the end of this number, very drained, which I thought meant I had skated it well. She just asked for some Visine. Then Daria came up to me and said, "Mom, why did you wrap your arm around your head when you were skating?"

It was the pose I had used when expressing my misery to God that Sergei was gone. I said, "You didn't like this pose?"

"No."

"Okay." I smiled, hugging her. "I'll never do it again."

Marina didn't talk to me much about the second number, the finale, in which I was skating for Sergei. She said for me to try to be beautiful, try to skate well, try for Sergei to smile. Try to skate as if to say thank you, Sergei, for having been my husband, friend, and partner. Remember me always as this beautiful, and I, of course, will remember you my whole life. Thank you for sharing yours with me.

When I skated this finale, I didn't feel so powerful. I did, however, feel relaxed and happy, even joyful. Scott was the first onto the ice, and he invited all the other skaters to join him. The costumes they were wearing were white, and everything looked so pure and clean and beautiful. Then I skated past them as if to say, Show me what Sergei and

Katia used to look like. That's when they assumed the poses that Sergei and I had done throughout our career. They held these poses until I got to the end and turned around, then the next time I passed, it was like I was telling them, Thank you for showing me Sergei and Katia one last time. Then I destroyed the poses with a wave of my hand.

I skated up to Scott, as if to ask, Can I skate as a single? I think of Scott, not as the king of skating so much as the god of skating. He's so natural both on and off the ice. I feel such high respect for him, that if I were to ask anyone for permission to skate, I'd ask him.

And then I skated a little, and bowed to the audience like in a Russian folk dance. But you know, I didn't feel comfortable with this number. I wanted everyone to skate more in the finale. I didn't want everyone looking at me. The show was for Sergei. It was his night.

I knew afterward that I was supposed to say something. I thought I should get a speech ready, but as soon as Scott handed me the microphone, I couldn't think of any words. I was later upset I didn't thank enough people. I should have mentioned more names. But what came out was approximately this:

> "I'm so happy that this evening happened, and I'm sad it's all over. I want to start it over again. I want to thank all of you, because I know I will not be able to

Heinz Kluetmeier

Skating for Sergei.

skate here if all of you did not come tonight. I'm so happy I was able to show you my skating. But I also want you to know that I skated today not alone. I skated with Sergei. It's why I was so good. It wasn't me."

I started to lose my composure when I began to thank the other skaters:

"I want to thank all you guys. You're the best. You're such a good friend. You're so good. Thanks, Scott. Thanks, everyone. Thanks, Sandra, Michael, Lee Ann. So many names. Thanks, United States. Thank you *so* much. And I want to introduce you to Sergei's mother. She came all the way from Moscow, first time to United States. And she gave me Sergei and I want her to . . ."

Anna took the microphone then, and I translated her thanks.

Then I thanked my own parents, who were sitting with Anna and Daria. Then I remembered what I had wanted to say: "I don't have enough words, but I also want to wish to all of you: Try to find happiness in every day. At least once, smile to each other every day. And say just one extra time that you love the person who lives with you. Just say, 'I love you.' It's so great. Okay? Thanks everyone. Goodbye."

Moving On

$\mathcal{T}$ ime, I have learned, is a doctor. I am finding that the good days increasingly outnumber the bad ones. My smiles come more naturally. My longing, while it remains, is less acute. It will always remain, but it's a room inside me that I no longer feel compelled to visit.

Skating has been the best medicine for me. I love being with the people; I like the training; I like the feeling of being physically tired after a long practice session. After Sergei died, I lost myself when I was so long off the ice. To come back to myself, I must skate. I cannot not skate.

It's more natural for me on the ice. It's terrible to say, but when I'm only living at home, when I'm only giving myself to my parents and to Daria, I can feel my strength slipping away. When I skate, it returns. My confidence returns. This is good for me, but it's also good for Daria. She sees that her mom is not weak, that she can do something well. She likes the way I skate, likes my costumes, likes the way I look on the ice. It's the best way for me to express my emotions. It's easier than to write, than to talk, than to think. I just skate the elements that I've been skating all my life, and if I can perform like I did the night of the tribute to Sergei, it's perfect.

Some performances go better than others. On the tour now, when I skate alone, I don't feel at all like I did when I skated in Hartford for Sergei. Scott Hamilton told me that night, "Fill up the ice with yourself." And I could. I felt huge, powerful, double strong.

Now it's like I never did that show. I don't feel I have something so special to share with the audience. I imagine them saying, "It's too bad she's skating alone." Or maybe, "It's nice to see her on the ice." These thoughts are always going through my head when I'm out there, which is distracting and disconcerting. I'm very aware that everyone's just watching me. I don't know where my eyes should go. I never had this contact, mental and visual, with the audience when I skated before. I only had contact with Sergei.

But I'm learning. I'll figure it out. I know, someday in the future, I'll coach. Not soon, I hope. But when I can't skate anymore. I have to tell someone the secrets I know about skating. It would be so great to help someone grow up to become a champion. Sergei and I did a coaching clinic once in Canada, and he could see a mistake and explain exactly what to do about it. All I did was translate for him. You have to have such patience to be a coach, and Sergei was definitely patient. You have to watch a program, see a million mistakes, but not let your student see on your face that there's a problem. Instead, you must say, it was good, only maybe try this one thing. And the next day it's another thing. And the next day another and another. Patience.

I would never want Daria to grow up to be a skater. I shouldn't write it like that. What I'd like is for her to have more options than only being a skater. I want her to understand computers, to understand business, to understand politics. I'll see to it she has more education than I had, that she spends more time in school than I did. I want her to be beautiful in the way my mother is beautiful — to be smart, strong, selfless, and have beautiful taste. I want her to be physically fit, which is why I'd like to see her involved in some kind of sport when she's young.

I want her to be whatever she wants to be. It's what I admire in Daria already. She knows what she wants, and she doesn't care what her mom thinks about the matter. She was born like this. Maybe she inherited this from Sergei. If she wants to be a skater, she'll be a skater. And then I will do what I can to help.

I think I'll be learning a lot of things from

Daria in the future. I already am learning from her. Sergei never taught me things. He protected me; he loved me; he took care of me; he comforted me. But it is only with his death that I start to learn about life. Only now has he started to teach me.

I am learning that life doesn't give everything to you. You also have to create your own future, your own opportunities. Before, my life consisted of training, skating, winning, moving to the United States, and living with the person I loved. Everything was too easy. The difficulties I encountered were trivial—not life-changing difficulties. They were things like the language barrier, taking care of airplane tickets, breaking in new boots, training. These were nothing. I am learning that life is more difficult than I thought.

Mostly, I'm learning about myself. It still hurts me to see couples that we knew. I ache inside when I see Nina and Viktor Petrenko, to know that Nina can hug Viktor anytime she wants, that they can always hold each other's hands. Nina's such a calm, reassuring presence, and sometimes I just want to lay my head on her shoulder, or someone's shoulder. I never wished to do this before with friends. With Sergei, I never thought about friends. I could see them, or not see them, for a long time.

Now I need to see friends. I never thought I'd learn to talk to people, to be interested in other people's lives. I was never very good about this.

But I've started to be a little more open with people. I'm interested to hear what they think about things. I've gotten to know my parents again, what they like to do, what they don't like. I'd forgotten these things. There are new things in life, and probably good things in life, that I am just now starting to discover.

So I am cautiously stepping into the future with my mind set on becoming, if not happier, at least wiser in life. My youth I am leaving behind. It will stay always with my precious Seriozha.

Epilogue

"My youth I am leaving behind.
It will stay forever with my precious Seriozha . . .

*L*ife does go on. This I have learned. Since MY SERGEI was completed, my days have been a mixed bag of painful times and wonderful times, gratifying moments and lonely ones. In all areas of my life, I have felt the support of so many people, and this has helped me to keep going and move forward.

My parents, more than anyone, have been there for me every step of the way. I am so thankful for their love and support. My mother is an incredibly wise and strong woman. We have become closer than ever—best friends. My father has been so different since Sergei's death. It's hard to explain, but he worries about whether I am strong enough to go on without Sergei. He didn't have to worry about me with Sergei. In his eyes, I am a little girl again. He is such a caring father and grandfather, and he loves having Daria around—she always brings a smile to his face.

Fortunately, my parents have been able to spend most of the winter with me in the States, and return to Russia in the summer. It is an enormous help for me while I am traveling, because Daria is attending school and that routine is important for her, especially as she gets older.

Daria is now five years old, and is a joy! She is growing up so fast, and talking, talking all the time—in Russian and in English. She speaks Russian in the house with my family and Russian-speaking friends, and English in school with her friends and all those in her life who speak English. She is very active and busy with Montessori school which she will attend for one more year before she starts kindergarten, and she is also taking gymnastics and skating lessons. It amazes me how smart she is. She loves to read and absorbs everything. She is much like Sergei in this way.

During the winter, between our "Stars on Ice" tour and competitions, I was on the road constantly and missed Daria's company so much. That's why her visits meant so much, not only to me, but to the rest of the cast. "Dasha Day" is what Scott Hamilton calls the first day of Daria's visits. Everyone becomes a kid again—there is a lot of laughter and even more hugs and smiles. Daria became very close to Kurt Browning this year—I guess because he is really a kid at heart.

Personally, I have adjusted to my life without

Sergei. Is there really any other choice? I believe Sergei is watching over us. If I need him, he is there. Although he is not with us physically, he is with us spiritually, in a way that's subtle, yet always comforting. Natalia, Sergei's sister, visited the States in November, 1996 and spent the first anniversary of Sergei's death with me in Lake Placid. We had a beautiful service at the Olympic Center, and I was very happy she could be there with me. It was important for her to see where her brother lived . . . and died. It was one of his wishes that Natalia visit the States one day, so her trip here had extra special meaning.

Professionally, I am skating as a singles skater, but it still doesn't feel quite right. I guess you could say that I am determined. Skating is what I know, and the thought of pairs skating with anyone other than Sergei does not seem to be an option at this point, so I have learned (and am still learning) how to skate without anyone to hold on to. At times it has been difficult. It was particularly hard during the competitions when I skated as a singles skater for the first time. I would get very nervous before I went out on the ice. My first competition was the Northwestern Mutual Life Championship, which was a team formatted event, so the pressure was not as great because our scores were based on the team's performance as a whole. The Russian Team placed fourth. My next event was the U.S. Pro in Albany, which was technically my first competition as a singles skater. I competed against

Kristi Yamaguchi and Katarina Witt. I had always admired the skating of these two champions and now I had to compete against them!! The pressure was intense. My mother, father and Daria were there, which helped a lot. Given the tough competition, I did surprisingly well and managed to come in second. Then came the Gold Championship. This format was simple—the top three Gold medal women and the top three Gold medal men. Oksana Baiul was injured, and I was the only one who could replace her. Although I was a two time Gold medalist, it wasn't in the singles category, but I agreed to compete. I must admit the prize money was very enticing—a one-million-dollar purse. So, once again I found myself competing against Kristi and Katarina and once again I placed second. I was so happy! And my confidence level was boosted. I was ready for more competitions. I had a very big support group cheering me on, which made all the difference in the world. Although I felt under a lot of pressure, I knew I had to compete if I was going to conquer my fears.

My programs were choreographed by Marina Zueva, who I continue to depend upon to create the most beautiful programs. The music she chooses and the way she choreographs always tells a story that corresponds with a period in my life and it is up to me to convey that story on the ice. I am forever grateful for Marina's support as well as the support of Galina Zmieskaia. Training in

Simsbury along with Victor Petrenko and Galina helps me prepare both physically and mentally for the competitions.

I felt pressure not only during the competitions, but also sometimes during the Stars on Ice tour. Some performances I would put so much unnecessary pressure on myself that I would end up in tears if I missed a jump. I always tried to remember Scott Hamilton's advice that I should just concentrate on my skating and not so much on the jumps.

This year, the Stars on Ice U.S. tour lasted for three months and traveled to 61 cities. The schedule was difficult and life on the road was tiring, but it almost didn't matter because I was so happy to be back with all of our friends. It was like I never left, except Sergei wasn't there.

It was a great group and in between traveling and shows, we managed to have fun. There weren't as many group activities this year as in the past due to the fast pace of the schedule, so I found myself spending more time alone, which was sometimes sad, but I managed to see quite a few movies and even read one or two English books. Our motto was "Day Off, Travel Day, Same Thing, Whatever." Gregg Maltby, our lighting director, had T-shirts with these words made up for everyone.

Obviously, the tone of the tour changed when Scott was diagnosed with cancer. His presence was missed in every way imaginable during th last ten shows, which we performed without him. Fortunately, his prognosis was always optimistic and Scott's attitude just as positive. The Stars on Ice group is very close and the love we have for one another helps us deal with the ups and downs of life. We called Scott every night from the show. One night, we even brought the cell phone out during the opening number so he could be with us.

Sergei's and my fans in every city were so amazing, so supportive. The beautiful cards, letters and gifts have meant so much to me and Daria. I think I will be sending thank-you notes for some time.

As I look ahead, my future seems very promising. I am working on a documentary of our lives for CBS-TV. It will be titled, "My Sergei" and should air some time either in Fall 1997 or soon after the new year. It is a very special project for me, just as writing this book was. The success of MY SERGEI has been overwhelming. I am so proud of the book.

I plan to compete again in Fall 1997 and tour with Stars on Ice in the U.S. and Canada next winter. There are a few other projects on the horizon, but I can't give all my secrets away. What I can tell you now is that the future seems less frightening to me, less sad than it once did and I approach it filled with hope and resolve and, always, with memories of my Sergei.

—Ekaterina
Summer, 1997